To renew or order library books visit
www.lincolnshire.gov.uk
You will require a Personal Identification Number.
Ask any member of staff for this

BREAD

BREAD

ERIC TREUILLE & URSULA FERRIGNO

Photography by
IAN O'LEARY

LONDON, NEW YORK, MELBOURNE, MUNICH, DELHI

NEW EDITION

Editors Shannon Beatty, Penny Warren
Managing Editor Stephanie Farrow
Senior Art Editor Rosamund Saunders
DTP Designer Sonia Charbonnier

ORIGINAL EDITION

Project Editor Julia Pemberton Hellums
Senior Editor Nicola Graimes
Editor David Summers
Project Art Editors Hilary Krag, Gurinder Purewall
Designer Rachana Shah
Senior Managing Editor Krystyna Mayer
Managing Editors Mary Ling, Susannah Marriott
Managing Art Editor Toni Kay
DTP Designer Karen Ruane
Production Manager Maryann Webster

First published in Great Britain in 1998
Revised edition published in Great Britain in 2004
Reissued in Great Britian in 2007 by
Dorling Kindersley Limited,
80 Strand, London WC2R 0RL
Penguin Group

A CIP catalogue record for this book is available
from the British Library.

ISBN: 978-1-4053-1996-6

Reproduced in Italy by GRB Editrice, Verona
Printed and bound in Singapore by
Star Standard

Discover more at
www.dk.com

CONTENTS

INTRODUCTION

In France and in Italy, where we come from, a meal is not a meal without bread. There, bread is taken very seriously. The daily visit to the bakery is a ritual that punctuates the rhythm of life. People choose their bread with special care and patronise the baker of their choice with an almost religious allegiance. It is said that the table is not laid until there is bread set on it. Bread is used to eat *with* as much as it is eaten: a piece of bread is used as a kind of secondary fork, and then is used to wipe the plate clean of every last morsel. Indeed culinary life, for many, begins with bread as mothers give their babies a hard crust to cut their teeth on.

All over the world, bread plays an important role in festivals and celebrations, traditions, and superstitions. Eric's father, like others of his generation, still marks the sign of the cross with the tip of his knife on the base of a loaf before he cuts it. Both of us clearly remember being warned as children not to place a loaf of bread top crust down on the table as it was sure to bring bad luck.

We were both privileged that our first experiences of making bread came early. Indeed, Eric's first contact with professional cooking was with bread; in his school holidays, he worked as a *mitron* – a baby baker – at *Le Fournil*, his uncle's *boulangerie* in South West France. Ursula remembers the hot summer evenings when her grandmother would light the wood-fired oven on the terrace of their family home in Campania. She recalls the sweet, yeasty fragrance of the seemingly magically growing dough and its soft, springy texture as she formed it into a thin round, for it was a family tradition that each person shape and top their own pizza.

When work drew us away from our homes to London, we were puzzled and shocked at the acceptance of mass-produced, inferior bread. It was our natural appreciation of bread with which we were raised that propelled us into baking bread at home for ourselves and then into teaching others how to do the same. Besides providing good food, something wonderful happens to your kitchen and your life when breadmaking becomes a regular activity. We hope that this book brings the same tremendous pleasure and satisfaction.

Eric   Ursula

THE FUNDAMENTALS OF BREADMAKING

AKING BREAD REQUIRES little more than a pair of hands, an oven, and patience. The recipe for success is simple: time and warmth are all it takes to transform a few basic ingredients into a springy, silky dough that bakes to a crackly, crusted loaf. It is like most things, easy when you know how, with practice making perfect. If we had to choose one single phrase that we feel is essential to breadmaking, it would be this: *bread is alive*. It is a living, growing entity, and above all, the product of its ingredients and its surroundings; it responds, just as we do, to its environment – "treat rising dough as if it were human" advises an old English farmhouse cookery book. While we advocate the use of scales, timers and thermometers, remember that observation is the baker's traditional tool. The more you make bread, the better your bread will be. Your mistakes are rarely irreversible (*see pages 162–163* for problem solving) or inedible.

ESSENTIAL INGREDIENTS AND TECHNIQUES

Flour is the main ingredient of most breads, accounting for about three-quarters of the finished loaf. The flour you choose will give your bread its individual character. Mass-produced, highly refined brands will make an honest loaf, but we urge you to seek out organic flours from independent mills to experience the taste and texture of truly great homemade bread.

The choice of flour affects not only the quality of the baked bread but also the breadmaking process. Flour will absorb more, or less, liquid according to the variety of wheat that it was made from, where it was harvested, and how it was milled. Such variables are compounded by the humidity in the air – on a damp day, flour will absorb less liquid than on a dry one.

The quantities of liquid given in the recipes can never be more than guidelines or general indications. Our mixing technique (*see pages 44–45*) suggests that you hold back a proportion of liquid and add it as needed. This method acts as a safeguard against overly wet dough and the consequent need to add extra flour, which upsets the balance between flour, salt, and yeast.

If you require a little more liquid than stated in the recipe, do not hesitate to add it; your aim is to produce a dough conforming to the consistency specified in the recipe, be it firm, soft, or wet. Observing and understanding the condition of your dough, and what it requires, is the key to successful breadmaking.

THE IMPORTANCE OF TEMPERATURE

A warm kitchen is a perfect place for making bread. Ideally, ingredients should be at room temperature before mixing – except the yeast, which should be dissolved at body temperature, 37°C (98.4°F). Summer heatwaves or even storing flour in a cool larder must be brought into the equation, and you may find it necessary to use cooler or warmer water to correct the balance – bearing in mind that yeast is killed by temperatures over 54°C (130°F).

In the days before central heating, people used to take their dough to bed with them! Less eccentric rising spots during cold weather include a warm bathroom, an oven with the pilot light on, and a position near, but not too close, to a radiator, open fire, or stove. Choose a glass or plastic bowl when rising dough; metal conducts heat over-efficiently and you might find the dough rising unevenly and drying on the side closest to a nearby heat source. Use temperature to control the baking timetable. Decrease the water temperature and leave the dough in a cool spot in order to slow down the rising process to fit in with your schedule; the refrigerator is ideal for all-day or overnight rising. Remember to allow a couple of hours for the dough to return to room temperature (*see page 50*).

THE JOYS OF BREADMAKING

Breadmaking works miracles on all levels. The slow, rhythmic kneading is therapeutic, opening up the lungs and rib cage, and releasing stresses and strains with gentle efficacy. Watch as the warmth and pressure of your hands brings the yeast to life and transforms a few commonplace ingredients into a growing dough. Everybody loves the smell of bread as it is being made. The yeasty fragrance of the rising dough permeates the kitchen, only to be superseded by the delicious aroma of the bread baking. Enjoy the process of breadmaking as well as the results.

BAKING AT HIGH ALTITUDES

Altitudes above 1,067m (3,500ft) have a low atmospheric pressure; this causes bread dough to rise and prove more quickly than is indicated in the book's recipes. No adjustments are need to the ingredients, but keep an eye on the dough and do not allow it to increase in volume more than is specified.

Breads that rise too quickly will not develop. To prevent this, allow the dough to rise twice (*see page 50–51*) before shaping.

At altitudes over 914m (3,000ft), increase the baking temperature by 15°C (59°F). This extra heat is needed to help form the crust in the intial stages of baking and to prevent the bread from over-rising during its final minutes in the oven.

SUCCESSFUL BREADMAKING

The golden rule for measuring all baking ingredients is to always stick to one system, never to mix and match. Both metric and imperial measurements are given in this book. It is imperative that you choose one system and use it throughout the recipe.

All spoon measurements are level: 1 teaspoon equals 5ml (⅙fl oz); 1 tablespoon equals 15ml (½fl oz). All eggs used in the book are large unless otherwise specified. Unsalted butter should always be used for breadmaking unless otherwise specified.

Make sure that all the ingredients used are at room temperature; be sure to take eggs, butter, and milk out of the refrigerator in good time.

A GALLERY
OF BREADS

A WORLD OF POSSIBILITIES IS REVEALED IN THIS
GALLERY OF BREADS, WHICH CELEBRATES A
TRULY UNIVERSAL FOOD. A MEAL IS NOT A MEAL WITHOUT
BREAD IN COUNTRIES AS DIVERSE AS ITALY, INDIA, MEXICO
AND FRANCE. A VARIETY OF TEXTURES AND TASTES ABOUNDS
TO DEFINE THIS GLOBAL CULINARY STAPLE. ILLUSTRATED
HERE IS A SELECTION OF BREADS FROM SOME OF THE
WORLD'S MOST FAMOUS BREADMAKING TRADITIONS.

FRENCH BREAD

AN 18TH-CENTURY FRENCH
BAKER KNEADS DOUGH IN
A WOODEN TROUGH

BREAD IS AT THE HEART of the French culinary experience, and once even defined social status – the long, elegant white *Baguette* was affordable only to stylish city dwellers and rustic breads, like *Pain de Campagne*, were staples of life in the country. Today, however, these country-style sourdough breads have captured the imagination of contemporary bakers from New York to Tokyo.

COURONNE

Bread shapes in France were often designed by the baker to satisfy the needs of his customers. The hole in the middle of this loaf makes it easy to carry over the arm like a shopping basket. As well as being practical, the loaf's shape increases the proportion of crust to crumb. *Recipe page 85.*

PAIN DE SEIGLE

In France, rye bread originated in mountainous regions like the Pyrenees and the Vosges, where it was a staple bread. Today, it is more often served in Parisian brasseries, thinly sliced and thickly buttered as an accompaniment to oysters. *Recipe page 93.*

PISTOLETS

These distinctively shaped rolls are traditional to Belgium and North Eastern France, where they are a Sunday breakfast treat. The characteristic indentation along the top of each roll is easily made with the handle of a wooden spoon. *Recipe page 79.*

PAIN DE CAMPAGNE

Made throughout France in innumerable shapes and sizes, *Pain de Campagne* varies by region as well as by baker. All these breads have thick, dark crusts liberally dusted with flour, giving them their characteristic two-tone appearance. *Recipe page 85.*

FOUGASSE

One of the 13 desserts traditional to a Provençal Christmas, *Fougasse* can now be bought all year round. This decorative, branch-shaped bread is flavoured and enriched with olive oil. Additional flavourings are often added to the bread dough – crisp bacon, chopped anchovies, or caramelized onions are very popular. *Recipe page 149.*

TORDU

From the Limousin, a rural region in the centre of France, *le tordu*, the "twist", is a popular shape. It is favoured by bread connoisseurs who prize crust as highly as crumb. *Recipe page 85.*

BAGUETTE

A crackly, golden crust and light, chewy interior are the signatures of this world-renowned, classic bread. The French say it is best to buy two loaves at a time, because one is always half eaten by the time it arrives home. *Recipe page 79.*

ITALIAN BREAD

**A 16TH-CENTURY
VENETIAN BAKERY**

AN ITALIAN TABLE is not dressed without bread. Renaissance paintings depict tables adorned with baskets of freshly baked bread and this appealing image is just as current today. Each region of Italy has its own distinctive style of cooking and breadmaking. The food of northern Italy is very rich and its ingredients reflect the historical wealth of this area. Delicate, light breads are made here. Southern Italian food is the food of a humbler people, and a luscious bread filled with cheese and vegetables serves as a meal in itself.

STROMBOLI

This southern Italian bread is stuffed with mozzarella, fresh herbs, and shallots. During baking, the generous filling erupts out of the indentations made in the bread's crust. Hence it is named after the volcanic island off the coast of Sicily. *Recipe page 106.*

SCHIACCIATA CON L'UVA

This Tuscan bread is made to celebrate the grape harvest. It is filled with wine-soaked raisins from the previous year's harvest and traditionally topped with the new season's grapes. *Recipe page 109.*

PANE DI RAMERINO

Enriched with olive oil and eggs, studded with raisins, and scented with fresh rosemary, this delicious bread is most commonly seen at the Tuscan breakfast table. *Recipe page 115.*

GRISSINI

From the city of Turin, these crispy breadsticks can be made as thin as a pencil or as fat as a cigar. Toppings vary from simple coarse salt to the seed or dried herb of your choice. *Recipe page 80.*

CIABATTA

Distinctive to the Emilia Romagna region of Italy, *Ciabatta* is now baked around the world. It was created as a light, airy textured bread to accompany the region's rich pasta and meat dishes. *Recipe page 90.*

BRITISH BREAD

**BAKING DAY IN A
19TH-CENTURY ENGLISH VILLAGE**

Whatever the shape, the typical British loaf has a soft, tender crumb and a crispy rather than crusty exterior, often liberally dusted with flour. Through the centuries, the unerring preference of the British people has been for loaves made from white wheat flour. Historically, fine white bread graced only the tables of the lords of the manor. There were separate guilds for bakers of white and brown breads and the saying "to know the colour of your bread" meant to know your place in society.

VICTORIAN MILK BREAD

Milk is an important ingredient in many British breads. The use of milk in place of water softens both the crumb and crust. This bread has a velvety texture and a golden, smooth exterior. Its fancy scroll shape is typical of the popular Victorian novelty breads. *Recipe page 76.*

BLOOMER

Half milk and half water are used to make this long, plump loaf with its crispy crust and light, tender crumb. A typically British shape, this deeply scored loaf dramatically expands or "blooms" during baking. *Recipe page 76.*

COTTAGE LOAF

The most distinctive British shape, the cottage loaf, is made by stacking a small, round loaf on top of a larger round and joining them by making a deep impression, traditionally formed with the baker's elbow. *Recipe page 73.*

GRANARY TIN LOAF

Granary bread is made with a blend of wheat and rye flours mixed with malted grains. It is the most recent addition to the family of British breads; its slightly sweet, nutty taste and moist texture make this loaf a favourite of both children and adults. *Recipe page 73.*

IRISH SODA BREAD

This everyday Irish bread is traditionally "baked" in a cast-iron pot set over the embers of an open fire. With a cake-like texture, this bread is made without yeast and is best eaten on the day it is baked. *Recipe page 141.*

SCOTS BAPS

Baps are soft, flat rolls made all over Great Britain, but are mostly associated with Scotland. There they are traditionally eaten at breakfast and called morning rolls. *Recipe page 77.*

EUROPEAN BREAD

THE BREADS OF EUROPE fall into two categories – the hearty country breads eaten daily and the lighter, richer, more refined breads reserved for feasts and celebrations. The traditional country breads were rarely made with wheat flour alone, but also incorporated a common staple of the region: rye in Germany, corn in Portugal, and potatoes in Hungary. Wheat flour was an expensive and precious commodity and these healthful additions provided nourishing bulk to the everyday European loaf.

A 19TH-CENTURY GERMAN BAKERY

PULLA

This saffron-coloured, cardamom-scented bread wreath is the traditional Christmas loaf of Finland. No longer restricted to festive occasions, it is now baked and eaten all the year round. *Recipe page 150.*

LANDBROT

The name of this crusty rye bread translates literally as "bread of the land", and it is one of the few breads that is baked throughout Germany; a rarity in this intensely regional country that boasts 400 different kinds of bread. *Recipe page 92.*

BROA

Originally from the Minho Province in the north of Portugal, this corn bread is now eaten all over the country. Maize grows profusely in Portugal and is used in many of the native dishes. *Recipe page 78.*

HUNGARIAN POTATO BREAD

In Hungary, potatoes are a staple commodity. This traditional bread uses potatoes to add moisture and substance to the loaf, which is subtly spiced with aromatic caraway seeds. *Recipe page 103.*

PARTYBROT

Guests can help themselves to this inviting German bread. It serves as the perfect centrepiece to a party's buffet table. *Recipe page 120.*

AMERICAN BREAD

**AN 18TH-CENTURY
COLONIAL BAKER**

Pioneers and homesteaders who settled the Americas brought the breadmaking traditions of their native countries with them and adapted these to suit the rustic conditions of their new home. Without the system of communal bakeries that had existed in Europe since the Middle Ages, they established an important tradition of home-baking that still exists today. North America is famous for its unique sourdoughs and quick breads, which are made without the traditional yeast leaveners.

SAN FRANCISCO SOURDOUGH

The origins of this bread date back to California's gold rush. Prospectors carried with them a mixture of flour and water kept in a packet strapped to their waists, which fermented to produce a leaven for this chewy, tangy bread. *Recipe page 86.*

FAN TANS

Native to New England, these fancy shaped rolls also go by the name Yankee Buttermilk. They have a light and airy texture that complements a hearty stew or roast. *Recipe page 121.*

PARKER HOUSE ROLLS

Soft rolls are a Sunday dinner staple all over America. This unique shape was created and popularized by the Parker House Hotel in Boston during the late 19th century. *Recipe page 118.*

CINNAMON RAISIN BREAD

Enriched with milk and flavoured with an inner whirl of raisins, this bread is an all-American breakfast favourite. Served toasted and topped with butter and cinnamon sugar, it is a fond childhood memory. *Recipe page 123.*

CORN STICKS

A heavy skillet was used by early settlers to cook corn bread on the hearth. Here, the quick bread batter is baked in a cast-iron mould that forms it into small ears of corn. *Recipe page 142.*

EASTERN BREAD

MEALTIMES IN THE MIDDLE EAST ALWAYS INCLUDE BREAD

THE IMPORTANCE OF BREAD in the Middle East cannot be overstated. In the Arab world, bread is revered as a gift from God and the staff of life itself. Honour is asserted with the vow "on my family's bread I swear to tell the truth"; contentment expressed by saying "his water jug is filled and his bread is kneaded". Bread is present at every meal, from the simplest snack to the grandest banquet, and indeed takes the place of cutlery throughout the region. The most common bread is flat with a hollow pocket in the middle, used for filling with salads, grilled meats, or any of the region's mouthwatering mezze.

LAVASH

It is said that *Lavash* originated in Armenia but it is also eaten throughout Lebanon, Turkey, and Syria. Rolled paper-thin, it is traditionally cooked in a large outdoor oven called a *tannur*. *Recipe page 134.*

PIDE

Recognized by its distinctive ridged pattern, golden crust, and topping of nigella seeds, *Pide* is traditionally prepared for the Muslim festival of Ramadan, when it is eaten to break the fast at sunset. It can be topped with fennel seeds instead of nigella seeds. *Recipe page 137.*

BARBARI

This light, crusty Persian bread is commonly served for breakfast in Iran, where it is topped with cheese and fresh herbs. When made with water instead of milk and sprinkled with sugar instead of seeds, the bread becomes a much-loved children's snack called *shirmal*. *Recipe page 136.*

PAIN TUNISIEN

With a tender crumb and crisp crust, this bread is made with semolina flour. Semolina is produced from durum wheat – a staple of North Africa that is widely used in breadmaking and to make the cracked grain, couscous. *Recipe page 135.*

PITTA BREAD

Pitta is the Greek name for a soft, oval- or round-shaped bread with a pocket-like hollow in the middle. It is made all over the region, where it also goes by its Arab name of *khubz*. *Recipe page 134.*

FESTIVE BREAD

PREPARING BREAD FOR A 17TH-CENTURY FESTIVITY

THE CUSTOM OF BAKING SPECIAL BREADS in honour of festive celebrations and religious holidays is an ancient one. In contrast to the plain, hearty loaves that comprise the traditional "daily bread", festive breads are usually made with the most expensive and highly prized ingredients – golden butter and eggs, aromatic spices and flavourings, and sweet, dried and candied fruits. These ceremonial breads are formed into traditional shapes that have special symbolic meanings. Some are now commonly served throughout the year and not just for an occasion.

PANETTONE

This rich, golden loaf from Milan is studded with sultanas and delicately perfumed with citrus peel. Its dome-shaped top is said to resemble the cupolas of the churches of its native Lombardy. *Panettone* is traditionally enjoyed at Christmas. *Recipe page 155.*

PAN DE MUERTO

Flavoured with orange and anise seeds, this sweet bread is baked on the Mexican Day of the Dead, when families honour their dead by visiting the graves with offerings of flowers and food. *Recipe page 152.*

BOLO-REI

Rich breads and cakes are traditional in southern Europe to celebrate the feast of the Epiphany on 6 January. This lavishly decorated "Kings' Cake", from Portugal, is shaped to symbolize the crowns of the Three Kings who are said to have visited the baby Jesus on this day. *Recipe page 154.*

CHALLAH

The golden, braided loaf traditional for the Jewish Sabbath is the most familiar shape. It is shown here coiled into a circle that symbolizes continuity, and is baked to celebrate the Jewish New Year, Rosh Hashanah. *Recipe page 150.*

BAKING ESSENTIALS

FLOUR, WATER, AND YEAST – THESE ARE THE ESSENTIAL INGREDIENTS OF BREADMAKING. WHEN BROUGHT TOGETHER WITH THE HELP OF YOUR HANDS, A FEW BASIC TOOLS, AND A HOT OVEN, THEY CAN BE TRANSFORMED INTO A WARM, FRAGRANT LOAF. THE BAKING ESSENTIALS ILLUSTRATED IN THIS SECTION REVEAL WHAT BREAD IS: A FEW SIMPLE INGREDIENTS ELEVATED BEYOND THEIR HUMBLE ORIGINS TO BECOME AN EVERYDAY MIRACLE.

WHEAT FLOURS

FLOUR IS A KEY INGREDIENT in all breads. Wheat flour is by far the most common type used in bread-making. The wheat kernel consists of three parts: bran, germ, and endosperm. The wheat bran is the husk that encloses the kernel, while the nutritious wheat germ is the seed of the future plant. The endosperm, the inner part of the kernel, is full of starch and protein. This high protein content makes wheat ideal for breadmaking. When dough is kneaded, the protein in the flour develops into gluten, an elastic substance that traps the carbon dioxide gas generated by the leavening agent, allowing the dough to rise.

THE MILLING PROCESS

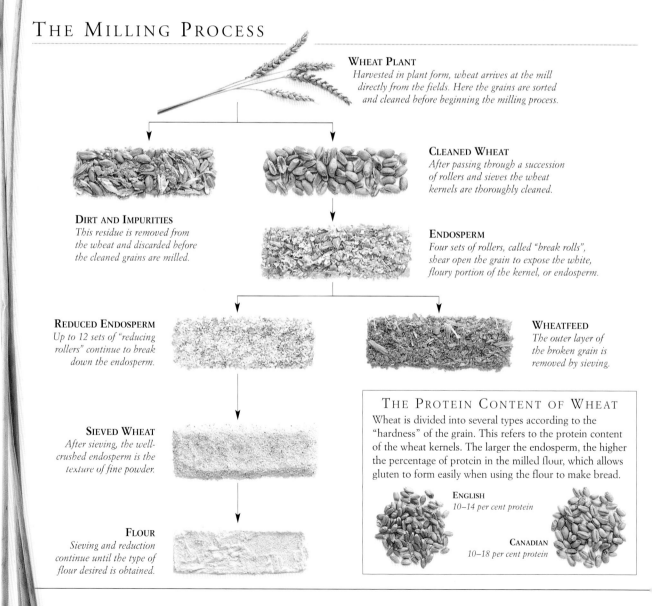

WHEAT PLANT
Harvested in plant form, wheat arrives at the mill directly from the fields. Here the grains are sorted and cleaned before beginning the milling process.

CLEANED WHEAT
After passing through a succession of rollers and sieves the wheat kernels are thoroughly cleaned.

DIRT AND IMPURITIES
This residue is removed from the wheat and discarded before the cleaned grains are milled.

ENDOSPERM
Four sets of rollers, called "break rolls", shear open the grain to expose the white, floury portion of the kernel, or endosperm.

REDUCED ENDOSPERM
Up to 12 sets of "reducing rollers" continue to break down the endosperm.

WHEATFEED
The outer layer of the broken grain is removed by sieving.

SIEVED WHEAT
After sieving, the well-crushed endosperm is the texture of fine powder.

THE PROTEIN CONTENT OF WHEAT
Wheat is divided into several types according to the "hardness" of the grain. This refers to the protein content of the wheat kernels. The larger the endosperm, the higher the percentage of protein in the milled flour, which allows gluten to form easily when using the flour to make bread.

ENGLISH
10–14 per cent protein

CANADIAN
10–18 per cent protein

FLOUR
Sieving and reduction continue until the type of flour desired is obtained.

TYPES OF WHEAT FLOUR

PLAIN FLOUR

A multi-purpose flour produced from a blend of hard and soft wheat. It can be used for bread and pastries but contains less protein and gluten than stronger flours made for breadmaking.

WHOLEMEAL FLOUR

Made from the complete wheat kernel with nothing removed, this flour makes a fuller flavoured, nutritious but denser loaf than plain flour. The extra bran hinders rising.

STRONG WHITE FLOUR

Also referred to as bread flour, this flour is milled from hard wheat that has a higher proportion of gluten than plain flour. This ensures an elastic dough and a lighter loaf.

COARSE SEMOLINA FLOUR

A coarse, gritty flour milled from the endosperm of durum wheat, which is one of the hardest varieties of wheat. It can be used in combination with plain flour for making bread.

FINE SEMOLINA OR DURUM FLOUR

Also referred to as semola di grano duro, *this high-gluten flour is made from the endosperm of durum wheat and is ground twice to produce a fine flour that makes it ideal for breadmaking.*

GRANARY FLOUR

A combination of wholemeal, white, and rye flours mixed with soft malted grains, this flour makes a textured loaf with a nutty, naturally sweet flavour. It is a popular breadmaking flour.

BROWN FLOUR

Also called wheatmeal, this flour contains most of the wheat grain's germ but has had some of the bran removed. It will produce a lighter finished loaf than wholemeal flour.

MIXING FLOURS

Experimenting with different combinations of wheat and non-wheat flours enables the home baker to create breads with special textures, flavours, and colours. The secret of mixing flours successfully is balance. See the selection of non-wheat flours on pages 30–31 and follow the guidelines given here to get the best results when combining flours:

Any mixture must always include some wheat flour. The protein content of wheat flour allows the development of gluten, which is critical for a well-risen bread.

Two-thirds strong white wheat flour combined with one-third non-wheat flour gives bread optimum volume and texture.

The greater the proportion of non-wheat flour, the more pronounced its effect on the flavour and texture of the bread.

If the proportion of non-wheat flour is increased, the dough will rise more slowly, creating a much denser finished loaf.

Different flours absorb water at varying rates. Sift flours together to assure an even distribution before adding liquid to them.

NON-WHEAT FLOURS

FOR CENTURIES VARIOUS DRIED GRAINS and roots have been ground and used to make bread. Most flours and meals come from cereal plants ground from seeds, including those made from rye, oats, barley, and corn. The seeds vary in shape and size, but all have a similar structure to the wheat kernel and are ground in the same manner. These flours produce breads with different flavours, textures, and nutritional values. Wheat flour, with its high gluten content, is preferable for risen breads. Low-gluten and non-gluten flours must be mixed with at least 50 per cent wheat flour to make a properly risen bread, but the addition of a few tablespoons of one of these flours will deepen a bread's flavour.

PRINCIPAL CEREAL GRAINS

RYE PLANT

GRAIN   FLOUR

RYE

Ground from cleaned grains, this flour inhibits gluten development. Even a small addition, mixed with wheat flour adds a distinctive tang to any bread. Dark rye flour contributes a strong flavour, while light rye flour is milder and paler.

OAT PLANT

GROUTS   PINHEAD OATS   FLOUR

OATS

Oats that have been cleaned and hulled are called oat grouts. Pinhead oats are grouts that have been cut into two or three pieces. Oat flour is ground from groats and is gluten-free. It adds rich flavour and texture to a bread.

BARLEY PLANT

PEARL BARLEY   FLOUR

BARLEY

Barley seeds with the bran removed are called pearl barley, which is eaten in soups and stews. Barley flour is ground from pearl barley and is gluten-free. Mixed with wheat flour it adds a sweet, earthy flavour.

CORN PLANT

KERNELS   COARSE MEAL   FINE MEAL

CORN

Dried corn kernels are ground into three textures of meal – coarse, medium (called polenta), and fine. All are gluten-free and have a distinctive corn flavour.

LOW-GLUTEN AND NON-GLUTEN FLOURS

PEOPLE WHO ARE INTOLERANT to wheat or gluten can use low- or non-gluten flours to make bread. However, since it is gluten that gives dough its elasticity and strength and allows it to rise, breads made exclusively with the flours shown here and opposite may have a dense, crumbly texture. When used in combination with wheat flour, these flours will contribute extra nutritional value and flavour to a bread. See page 29 for tips on mixing wheat and non-wheat flours.

SPELT FLOUR
A flour rich in nutrients with a slightly nutty flavour. It is low in gluten, but high in protein, which makes it a digestible substitute for wheat flour in breadmaking for the gluten-intolerant.

MILLET FLOUR
This flour is low in gluten but very rich in protein, vitamins, and minerals, with a distinctively sweet flavour. It is used mostly in combination with wheat flour for bread.

BROWN RICE FLOUR
Milled from the whole rice grain, this flour is completely gluten-free. When blended with wheat flour, it contributes a dry texture and a sweet, nutty taste to a bread.

POTATO FLOUR
This gluten-free flour is made from cooked, dried, ground potatoes. Mostly used as a thickener, when combined with other flours, it produces a moist crumb in breads.

GRAM FLOUR
Made from ground chickpeas, this gluten-free flour is also, unsurprisingly, known as chickpea flour. Just a small proportion gives a rich flavour to leavened flat breads and other savoury dishes.

QUINOA FLOUR
Quinoa contains more protein than any other grain as well as all eight essential amino acids. It is gluten-free and when mixed with wheat flour it is a rich source of nutrients for bread.

CORNMEAL FLOUR
Most commonly used in American quick and non-yeast breads, this gluten-free flour can be combined with white flour to make bread with a gritty, coarse texture and a sweet, corn flavour.

BUCKWHEAT FLOUR
This flour is ground from the seeds of a plant native to Russia and is not akin to the wheat plant, but is in fact gluten-free. The grey-brown flour has a distinctive bitter flavour.

INGREDIENTS

BREADMAKING involves just a few simple ingredients, each of equal importance. Leavens cause a dough to rise by creating bubbles that expand the gluten strands in the dough. This is not possible without the presence of liquid, which transforms the flour and yeast into a dough. Sugar encourages the dough to rise, while salt inhibits the process. Enrichments, such as butter, oil, and eggs, allow the baker to vary a bread's flavour, texture, and appearance.

LEAVENS

YEASTS

YEAST IS THE COMMONLY USED LEAVEN in breadmaking. It is a living organism that converts the natural sugars in flour to gases. Fresh yeast is available on request from the bakery section of most supermarkets. It should be used within 1–2 days of purchase as its freshness can be unpredictable. Dried and easy-blend yeast are more concentrated and long-lasting; use by their sell-by-date.

CHEMICAL LEAVENS

WHEN MOISTENED with liquid, baking powder and baking soda instantly create air bubbles, which act as the leaven in a quick bread batter. This requires the loaf to be baked immediately. Cream of tartar is used in combination with baking soda.

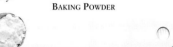

BAKING POWDER

BAKING SODA

CREAM OF TARTAR

DRIED YEAST
Activate in tepid water before adding to the flour.

FRESH YEAST
Dissolve in tepid water before adding to the flour.

EASY-BLEND YEAST
Sprinkle into the flour; activate by adding liquid.

CHEMICAL LEAVENERS
These are used as the raising agents in the Quick Bread recipes (see pages 138–145).

LIQUIDS

WATER
The primary liquid used to dissolve yeast and to form a bread dough.

MILK
Creates a tender crumb when used in place of water.

LIQUID IS FUNDAMENTAL to breadmaking. Liquid activates the yeast when it is at the correct temperature, and it gives life to the flour by transforming it into a dough. For a loaf with an extra tender crumb, water can be replaced with milk. Buttermilk and yogurt can be used interchangeably to produce a bread with a moist, almost cake-like texture. Extra liquid can be added to a dough when it is needed to achieve the dough consistency specified in a recipe.

YOGURT
Adds a tangy flavour and a moist texture to a bread.

BUTTERMILK
Can be made from skimmed milk and lemon juice (see page 164).

SALTS

SALT IS USED in most bread recipes to control the rate of fermentation and to give flavour. The presence of salt in a dough inhibits fermentation, which strengthens the developing gluten. This results in a bread with a stable crumb, a long shelf-life and more taste than breads made without it.

FINE SALT
Dissolves well and is best for making bread dough.

COARSE SALT
Sprinkled over an unbaked loaf this makes a flavourful topping.

ENRICHING INGREDIENTS

FATS ARE THE PRIMARY enriching ingredients which when used in a bread recipe change the character of the resulting dough. The fat coats the gluten strands, creating a barrier between the flour and yeast, which slows down both the fermentation and the rising time. In a recipe calling for a large addition of fat, the enriching ingredient or ingredients will be incorporated into the dough after an initial period of rising. In general, breads made with enrichments have a soft, tender crumb and become more cake-like the higher the proportion of butter and eggs added. Select only the best-quality enrichments for breadmaking.

VEGETABLE OIL
Use a light, neutral oil like sunflower.

BUTTER
Use only unsalted creamery butter when enriching a bread dough.

SUGARS

SUGAR CAN ACCELERATE the fermentation process of bread dough by providing additional food for an active yeast culture. However, modern yeasts do not need sugar to become active. Sugar is no longer a necessary ingredient in bread recipes, but it is used to enhance a bread's flavour, texture, and crust colour.

MALT EXTRACT
Made from malted wheat or barley, this encourages active yeast.

MOLASSES
Adds a sweet, slightly bitter flavour and a dark golden colour to bread.

GRANULATED SUGAR
The most commonly used sugar for making bread.

HONEY
Runny honey melts well when used for bread.

OLIVE OIL
Use a quality olive oil with a fruity fragrance and distinctive flavour.

EGGS
Choose fresh eggs with undamaged shells for making enriched doughs

EQUIPMENT

THE EQUIPMENT AND TOOLS required for breadmaking are as simple as the essential ingredients. The basic equipment list needed to make most of the breads in this book includes accurate scales, measuring jug and spoons, a large glass bowl, wooden spoon, tea towel, baking sheet, sharp blade, and an oven.

The remaining equipment shown will help you to tackle additional skills and special recipes. Be sure that you have a large, clean surface to work on that allows you plenty of room to move around; a marble slab, plastic board, or wooden table is best. Although a bare counter top is also fine, avoid tiles because the dough can stick to the grout.

MEASURING

BREADMAKING SHOULD BEGIN with careful measuring. For the best results, it is essential that the ingredients are in correct proportion to one another. When following a recipe it is important to use one system of measurement, either metric or imperial, throughout. These are not interchangeable systems. Before using scales check that the needle is on zero when they are empty. When using a measuring jug, place it on a flat surface and always bend down to pour the liquid at eye level.

MEASURING JUG
A jug with clearly marked units is important for measuring liquids.

MEASURING SPOONS
Always level off ingredients in measuring spoons.

SCALES
Accurate scales are essential for weighing small amounts.

MIXING AND RISING

CHOOSE GLASS OR PLASTIC bowls and wooden spoons. Metal bowls and spoons react with yeast, creating a metallic aftertaste in the dissolved yeast mixture. It is also advisable to avoid metal bowls for rising since they conduct heat, causing dough to rise too quickly. To prevent a dry crust from forming on a dough, cover the bowl with a clean tea towel during rising and proving.

GLASS BOWLS
These offer an all-round view and withstand vigorous use.

WOODEN SPOON
Essential for mixing yeasted batter.

GLASS JAR
Useful for making and storing sourdough starters (see page 43).

TEA TOWELS
Use to cover doughs during rising and proving, and to wrap soft-crusted breads warm from the oven.

OTHER HELPFUL TOOLS

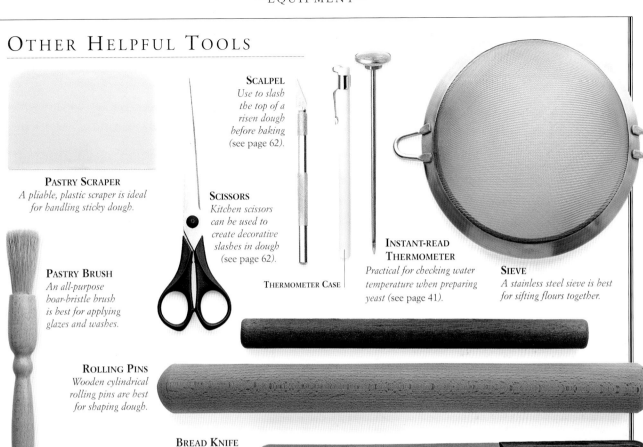

PASTRY SCRAPER
A pliable, plastic scraper is ideal for handling sticky dough.

PASTRY BRUSH
An all-purpose boar-bristle brush is best for applying glazes and washes.

SCALPEL
Use to slash the top of a risen dough before baking (see page 62).

SCISSORS
Kitchen scissors can be used to create decorative slashes in dough (see page 62).

THERMOMETER CASE

INSTANT-READ THERMOMETER
Practical for checking water temperature when preparing yeast (see page 41).

SIEVE
A stainless steel sieve is best for sifting flours together.

ROLLING PINS
Wooden cylindrical rolling pins are best for shaping dough.

BREAD KNIFE
A serrated knife will penerate a hard crust and slice through bread cleanly.

APPLIANCES

ELECTRICAL EQUIPMENT can be useful for mixing and kneading bread doughs. While a food processor ensures thorough mixing and partial kneading of a dough, a heavy-duty mixer allows the baker to develop the full elasticity of a dough through constant kneading for a longer period of time. However, electric mixers and processors can overwork and overheat the dough when set on a high speed. See pages 66–67 for tips on how best to use them.

FOOD PROCESSOR

HEAVY-DUTY MIXER

BAKING

AFTER THE INGREDIENTS HAVE BEEN CAREFULLY MEASURED and mixed to the proper consistency, the final stages of breadmaking also require the same careful attention. Preheat the oven in advance and use an oven thermometer to check its accuracy. A kitchen timer ensures that you keep track of the baking time, as well as the rising and proving times. Heavy-gauge baking tins and trays are best, since they resist buckling in the oven at high heats and prevent loaves from burning at the bottom.

KITCHEN TIMER
A clearly marked kitchen timer with a loud alarm will ensure accurate baking, rising, and proving times.

OVEN THERMOMETER
A thermometer will detect any variations in oven temperature (see page 64).

CORN STICK PAN
Each of this cast iron tray's depressions shapes a single serving of corn bread.

LOAF TIN
A 1kg (2lb) tin made from medium-weight metal is most frequently used in this book.

TERRACOTTA TILES
These help to radiate heat evenly and retain moisture in the oven, producing superior, thick-crusted, free-form breads (see page 63).

WATER SPRAY
A fine-spray nozzle is advisable for adding moisture to the oven while a bread is baking. Avoid spraying the oven light or heating elements directly (see page 63).

MUFFIN TIN
Use a non-stick, American-style muffin tin with deep cups in muffin recipes.

BREAD BOARD
Wooden boards are best for slicing bread since they are kind to the serrated blade of a bread knife.

BAKING SHEET
Use a heavy-duty, non-flexible, metal baking sheet for free-form loaves and rolls.

BRIOCHE MOULDS
The sloping sides of these classic moulds induce a maximum final rise and height during baking.

WIRE RACK
Use a wire rack to cool breads in order to prevent a soggy bottom crust (see page 65).

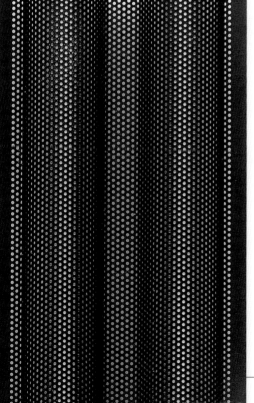

FRENCH BAGUETTE TRAY
This perforated tray ensures an even heat throughout baking, resulting in a crisp, golden outer crust.

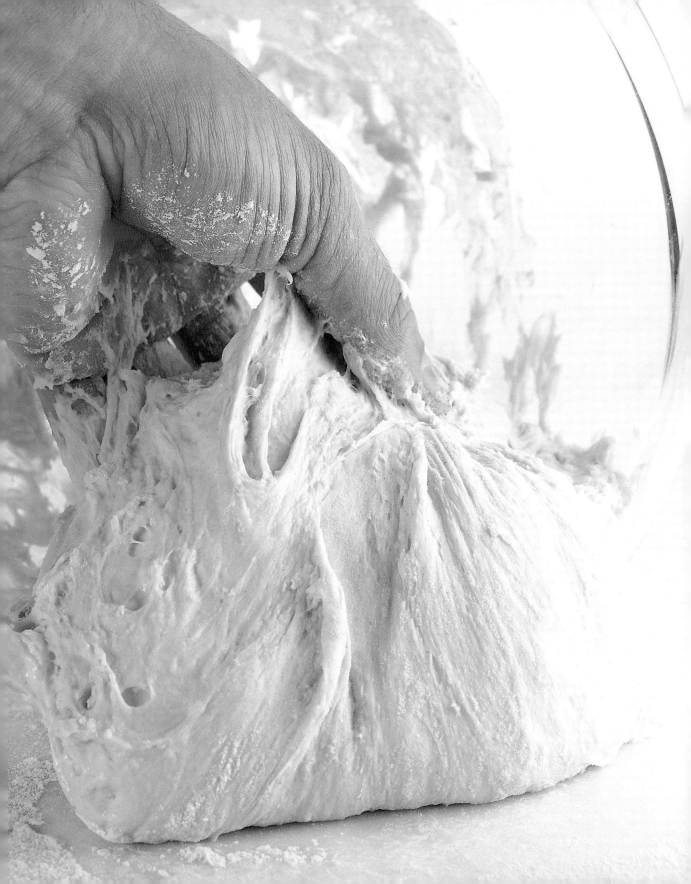

BASIC
TECHNIQUES

THE BASIC TECHNIQUES OF MAKING BREAD ARE

NOT COMPLICATED OR DIFFICULT TO FOLLOW.

SUCCESSFUL BREADMAKING, HOWEVER, REQUIRES TIME

AND PATIENCE – TRY NOT TO RUSH EACH STAGE. USE

THIS SECTION TO LEARN, FEEL, AND OBSERVE THE

PROCESSES THAT TRANSFORM BASIC INGREDIENTS

INTO A FINISHED LOAF. THIS IS YOUR HANDYWORK;

THE JOYS OF MAKING YOUR OWN BREAD BEGIN HERE.

HOW TO BEGIN

PRECISE PROPORTIONS and accurate quantities of leavener, water, and flour form the foundation upon which all good bread is based. The leavener, or rising agent, is the key to transforming simple ingredients into a risen bread. In this book, yeast, in either fresh or dried form, is the most commonly used leavener.

Yeast is a living organism, which relies on the sugar and starch present in flour to live and grow. Yeast produces carbon dioxide gas as it grows; this gas causes the bread dough to rise. Once activated in water, yeast will live for up to 15 minutes before it must be added to flour, the food source it requires to stay alive.

MEASURING THE INGREDIENTS

ACCURACY IS CRUCIAL when making bread. Use a kitchen scale clearly marked in metric or imperial measurements for weighing flour and other ingredients. Follow either metric or imperial measurements throughout the recipe. These two types of measurement are not interchangeable.

Choose one and stick with it throughout the recipe. Weigh all the ingredients carefully before you begin. Use a jug with clearly marked units for measuring liquids. Place on a flat surface and bend down to eye level with the measured mark to pour into the jug.

PREPARING THE YEAST

BOTH DRIED AND FRESH YEAST must be dissolved in tepid water to activate. This should be done just before adding the yeast to the flour. Avoid using metal bowls or utensils to prepare the yeast. Metal will sometimes impart an aftertaste to a yeasted mixture.

USING EASY-BLEND YEAST

TO USE EASY-BLEND YEAST, sprinkle it directly on to the flour. The yeast will activate once the liquid has been added. The standard method of mixing the dough must be followed since easy-blend yeast cannot be used with the sponge method (*see page 44–45*).

USING DRIED YEAST

1 Sprinkle dried yeast granules into a small, glass bowl containing tepid water; leave to dissolve for 5 minutes.

2 Once the yeast has dissolved stir the mixture with a wooden spoon. The yeast mixture is now ready to be added to the flour.

Granules will float on the surface and then sink

Foam indicates that the yeast has been activated

USING FRESH YEAST

1 Crumble the fresh yeast using a wooden spoon in a small, glass bowl and add the water to it. As a general rule, the amount of water added to dissolve the yeast will be about a quarter of the water specified in the recipe.

2 Use a wooden spoon to cream the yeast until it dissolves in the water and forms a smooth, thoroughly blended paste. The yeast mixture is now ready to be added to the flour.

WATER TEMPERATURE

The ideal temperature for preparing yeast is 37°C (98.4°F). The easiest method for achieving this is to mix two-thirds cold tap water with one third boiling water. The water should be comfortable to the touch – not too hot, but not cool. An instant-read thermometer provides a fail-safe method of checking the water temperature (*see page 35*).

As a living organism, yeast is very sensitive to temperature. The temperature of the liquid you use to dissolve the yeast and to make the dough is crucial: too hot and the yeast is killed; too cool and its growth is inhibited.

Cool water can be helpful when conditions in the kitchen are extremely warm and you wish to slow down the rising process. Adding cool water to the yeast will inhibit the rate of fermentation, allowing the bread to rise at a normal rate when the room temperature is above normal.

USING A STARTER

STARTERS OFFER AN ALTERNATIVE METHOD of preparing the yeast before mixing a bread dough. A portion of the yeast is prepared and then combined with water and flour. This mixture is then left to ferment for between two hours and five days, which results in a bread with an open, airy texture and a superior flavour.

Breads made with a starter require advance planning because additional time is needed to allow the starter to ferment. Once the starter has fermented it is ready for the mixing step (*see pages 44–45*). The main difference between the starter methods described here is time; the ingredients are the same – flour, water, and yeast.

MAKING A STARTER

ANY BREAD CAN BE MADE with a starter. Simply mix some of the flour, water, and yeast together into a thick batter, and leave to ferment at room temperature. The proportions of ingredients and the timing depend upon the recipe. The timing varies from two hours for a French *poolish* (*see page 84*) to thirty-six hours for an Italian *biga* (*see page 84*).

1 In a non-metalic bowl, combine the amount of flour, water, and prepared yeast specified in the recipe. Mix with a wooden spoon to form a thick, yet pliable batter.

The mixture should be thick, but not too stiff

2 Cover the bowl with a tea towel, and leave the starter to ferment at room temperature for the amount of time specified in the recipe. The mixture will start to bubble and have a mild, yeasty fragrance.

3 The starter is now ready to be mixed with the remaining ingredients. Add the starter, and any additional yeasted water specified in the recipe, to the well formed in the flour. Mix the ingredients together as directed in the recipe (*see pages 44–45*).

CREATING AND FEEDING A SOURDOUGH STARTER

A TRADITIONAL SOURDOUGH STARTER is made with a flour and water paste that is left to ferment by wild, airborne yeast. Here, some yeast is added to encourage the fermentation process. Once established, a sourdough starter can be kept indefinitely in the refrigerator. The longer a starter is kept, the better the flavour of the baked bread. If you do not make bread regularly it is important to "feed" the starter every two weeks. To do this, stir the starter, discard half, and replace with an equal amount of water and flour.

1 In a large glass jar, sprinkle or crumble the yeast into the water; leave to dissolve for 5 minutes. Stir in the amount of flour specified in the recipe. Cover the jar with a tea towel (do not seal it) and ferment at room temperature for at least 48 hours and up to 5 days. The starter will become a loose, frothy batter. Use immediately or refrigerate for up to 2 weeks.

The fermentated starter is ready to use when it has become a loose batter

2 After using a portion of the starter, replace it with an equal amount of flour and water to keep it active for the next time you make bread. For example, if a recipe calls for 250ml (8fl oz) starter, after removing this amount stir 125g (4oz) flour and 125ml (4fl oz) water into the remaining contents of the jar. Ferment at room temperature for 12–24 hours before refrigerating.

OLD-DOUGH METHOD

A piece of "old dough" can also be used as a leavening agent. Instead of making a flour and yeasted water batter, simply incorporate a piece of dough saved from a previous batch of plain bread dough into your new batch of bread dough. Old dough can be made from scratch (*see page 86*) and kept wrapped in the refrigerator for up to two days before using, or freezing. Alternatively, when making a plain bread remove a walnut-sized piece of dough after the rising period. Wrap loosely in greaseproof paper and foil, allowing room for the dough to expand, and refrigerate or freeze. To use the dough, if frozen, thaw in the refrigerator overnight, then leave it to sit at room temperature for a minimum of two hours.

Wrapped properly, old dough will keep in the freezer for up to 6 months

MIXING

THE PRIMARY OBJECTIVE of mixing is to combine the basic ingredients into a soft, pliable dough ready for kneading. The quantity of liquid required will often vary according to the type of flour used, as well as the level of humidity and temperature on the day of breadmaking. A little less, or a little more, liquid than the recipe states may be required. Add extra liquid one tablespoon at a time;

it is best to err on the side of too soft than too dry. Take note of the consistency of the dough described in each recipe and add additional liquid accordingly. The sponge method adds a period of fermentation (specified in the recipe) to mixing. This results in a bread with a lighter crumb and a less yeasty flavour. Techniques for mixing additional ingredients into the dough are illustrated in the recipe section.

1 In a large bowl, combine the flour and salt. Use a wooden spoon to form a well. Add the yeasted water and any starter (*see pages 42–43*) to the well. If the recipe requires the ingredients to "sponge", refer to the method illustrated below.

2 Use a wooden spoon to draw in the flour from the sides of the bowl, a little at a time, to combine with the yeasted water in the well until a stiff paste is formed.

SPONGE METHOD

FOLLOW STEP 1 above, then draw enough of the flour from the sides of the bowl into the yeasted liquid to form a soft paste (*see left*) when mixed thoroughly.

COVER THE BOWL with a tea towel and leave for 20 minutes, or longer if specified in the recipe, until the paste is frothy and has expanded slightly in volume (*see left*). Proceed to step 3, opposite. ▶

3 Gradually pour in half of the remaining liquid while mixing in the remaining flour from the sides of the bowl. As the water is added, the texture of the combined ingredients will change from a crumbly mixture to a shaggy, slightly sticky mass that will begin to come away from the sides of the bowl and form into a ball (*see below*). Add the rest of the water, as needed, to achieve the consistency specified in the recipe. The dough should remain soft and should not be too dry before it is transferred to a floured surface for kneading (*see pages 46–47*).

KNEADING

ESSENTIAL FOR AN OPEN-TEXTURED, full-flavoured bread, kneading performs a crucial function in preparing a dough to rise. First, it completes the mixing process by distributing the activated yeast throughout the dough. Continued kneading then allows the flour's proteins to develop into gluten, which gives dough the ability to stretch and expand.

Starches are broken down to feed the yeast, which creates bubbles of carbon dioxide gas. These bubbles cause the dough to rise. The actions shown are a guide to kneading a basic dough. Specific instructions, such as kneading a soft, wet dough (*see page 88*) or kneading coarse ingredients into a dough (*see page 99*), are demonstrated in the recipe section.

1 To begin kneading, shape the dough by folding one half over the other, bringing the top half towards you. Keep a little additional flour at the side to lightly dust the dough as you knead should it become difficult to handle. Use this extra flour sparingly.

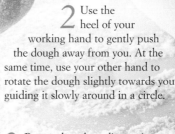

2 Use the heel of your working hand to gently push the dough away from you. At the same time, use your other hand to rotate the dough slightly towards you, guiding it slowly around in a circle.

3 Repeat these kneading actions, gently folding, pushing, and rotating the dough continuously for approximately 10 minutes, or until the dough achieves a firm touch, silky smooth surface, and elastic texture. Take time to work the dough slowly and firmly, but do not use excessive force. The dough will gradually become more elastic and easier to knead. Shape the dough into a ball for rising (*see pages 50–51*).

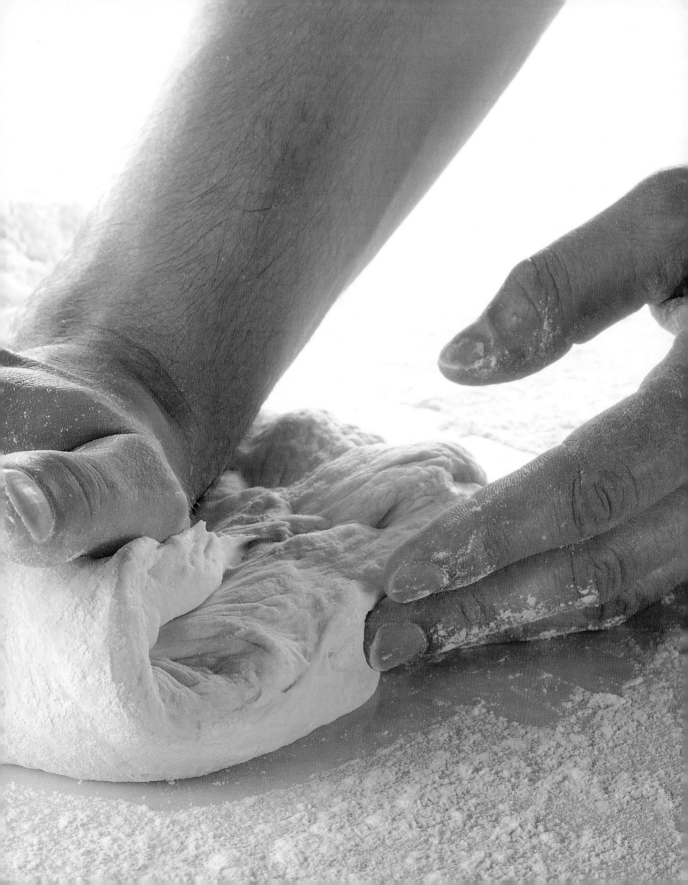

USING APPLIANCES

A FOOD PROCESSOR or heavy-duty electric mixer can be used as an alternative to mixing and kneading bread dough by hand. When using a food processor, check the capacity of your machine and, if necessary, divide the ingredients evenly so that you can mix and knead the dough in batches. Some kneading by hand will also be necessary. Bread dough can be made entirely in a heavy-duty electric mixer by using the mixing paddle to mix and the dough hook to knead. Be careful not to overwork the dough – high speeds stress the dough, causing it to rise incorrectly. Make use of the pulse button or low-speed setting on each appliance.

USING A FOOD PROCESSOR

1 Before starting, always fit the machine with a plastic dough blade. A metal blade will stress and overheat the dough.

2 Put the flour and any other dry ingredients into the work bowl; pulse to mix. With the machine running, pour in the yeasted water, followed by half of the remaining liquid. If using a starter, as specified in the recipe, add it to the work bowl at this point.

3 Add the rest of the water and continue to run the machine until the dough starts to form into a ball. Then leave the dough to rest in the machine for 5 minutes. Process the dough to knead for a further 45 seconds. Turn the dough out on to a lightly floured work surface and continue to knead by hand until smooth and elastic, about 3–5 minutes. Leave the dough to rise (*see pages 50–51*).

The dough should be firm and sticky before kneading by hand

HANDY TIPS

• *Use slightly cool water to dissolve the yeast to counterbalance the heat generated by the machine.*

• *After processing the dough in batches, turn them out on to a lightly floured work surface. Knead them together to form one piece of dough. Continue to knead until the dough is smooth and elastic.*

• *Use the pulse button often to prevent the machine from over-heating the dough. Do not run the machine continuously for more than 30 seconds at a time.*

USING A HEAVY-DUTY MIXER

1 Dissolve the yeast or make a starter as specified in the recipe and place directly in the mixing bowl. Use the paddle attachment to mix in half of the flour on low speed, then add the remaining liquid ingredients to the bowl.

2 Once the mixture forms into a loose batter, remove the paddle. Replace it with the dough hook. With the machine running, gradually add the remaining dry ingredients to the mixer.

3 Continue adding the dry ingredients until the dough pulls away from the sides of the bowl. Increase the speed to medium and work the dough until smooth and elastic, about 8–10 minutes. If the dough climbs up the hook, stop the machine, push it back down, and continue. Remove the dough from the mixer bowl to rise (*see pages 50–51*).

The dough will collect around the hook as it is kneaded

— HANDY TIPS —

• *Only use an electric mixer with a proper dough hook for kneading. A mixer with only paddle and whisk attachments is not equipped for breadmaking.*

• *An electric mixer is particularly helpful for kneading very stiff doughs, as well as doughs with enrichments and flavourings added to them.*

• *Check the recipe for the dough consistency required. Add extra water, if needed, 1 tablespoon at a time.*

RISING & KNOCKING BACK

THE SPEED OF RISING depends on certain factors, such as temperature and humidity, as well as the integral elements of a recipe, such as the type of flour and the method of leavening (that is, with or without a starter). On a warm, humid day dough should rise more quickly than on a cold, dry one; however, the exact effect of temperature can be difficult to predict. Rising times become more predictable only after years of experience with the same bread recipes. The novice baker might find it difficult to tell when the dough has doubled in size; use the test described in step 3 to help check the progress. If the dough over-rises see page 163 for a remedy.

RISING

1 Place the kneaded dough in a lightly oiled, glass or ceramic bowl large enough to allow the dough to double in size. Metal containers should be avoided since they can conduct heat, causing the dough to rise too quickly. Cover the bowl with a tea towel and leave to rise in a cool to normal, draught-free room.

RISING THE DOUGH IN THE REFRIGERATOR
This method allows breadmaking to be split into two stages, and is therefore useful for those with busy schedules. Place the dough in a deep, glass bowl that will allow it to expand, brush with oil, and cover tightly with clingfilm. To achieve a complete rise, refrigerate for at least eight hours. After rising, remove it from the refrigerator. Leave it at room temperature for two hours before proceeding to the shaping stage.

2 Leave the dough to rise until doubled in size. For most doughs this will take 1–2 hours. Wholegrain bread doughs and enriched bread doughs will take longer to rise. The slower a dough rises the more chance there is for it to develop flavour and texture. Do not allow the dough to over-rise.

Air bubbles will appear on the surface of a completely risen dough

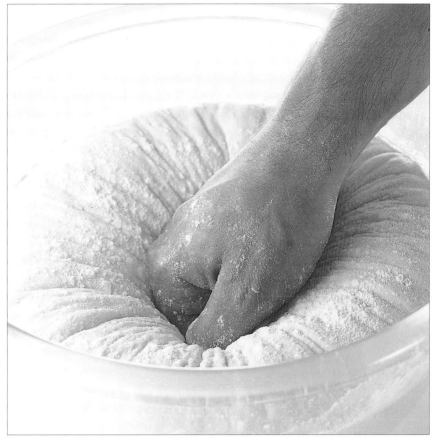

3 To ensure that rising is complete, test the dough by gently pressing with a fingertip. When rising is complete the indentation made will spring back gradually. If the dough is under-risen the indentation will spring back at once. If the dough is over-risen the finger will create a permanent mark that will not spring back at all (*see page 163*).

KNOCKING BACK

ONCE THE DOUGH has risen completely, knock back or deflate the dough by pressing down with your knuckles. Turn the dough out of the bowl on to a lightly floured work surface.

CHAFING

FORM THE DOUGH into a ball by cupping your hands gently around it. Apply a light, downwards pressure to the sides, while simultaneously rotating the dough continuously in a steady, clockwise motion. Continue until the dough is formed into an even, round shape. This action is called chafing. Some recipes specify an extended chafing time at this point. Otherwise, allow the dough to rest for 5 minutes, then proceed to the shaping stage.

Cup the dough gently with your hands

SHAPING & PROVING

AFTER A DOUGH HAS BEEN knocked back and rested, it is ready to be shaped. The techniques on the following six pages illustrate how to form the basic loaf shapes that are most frequently called for in the recipe section. Each stage of the shaping process requires careful attention – handle the dough gently and avoid over-shaping or excessive reshaping. Apply pressure evenly and allow the dough to rest if it begins to resist or tighten. Transfer the shaped loaf to a prepared baking sheet to prove (*see page 57*). Proving allows the dough to rise for a final time before baking. Avoid over-proving the dough; use the recommended test to check its progress.

SHAPING A LONG LOAF

1 Flatten the dough with the lightly floured palm of your hand to expel any gas bubbles. Keep the dough in a round shape by exerting pressure evenly. Take one end of the dough and fold it into the centre. Press gently to seal the fold.

2 Fold the other half of the dough into the centre, so that the two folds overlap along the middle of the loaf. Gently press along the length of the outer seam, using the lightly floured palm of your hand to seal the two folds together.

3 Use the thumbs of both hands to create an indentation in the centre of the dough. Before bringing the top half towards you, rest your fingertips along the top of the dough and give a firm, short push forwards. This action tightens the interior of the dough and gives an even-textured crumb when the bread is baked.

Press down into the centre of the dough and fold one half over the other

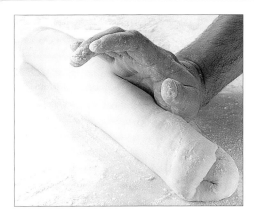

4 Gently press down with the palm of your hand along the seam to seal the fold. Place the dough seam-side down. Press evenly with the palms of both hands and roll the dough backwards and forwards to achieve the desired length as specified in the recipe.

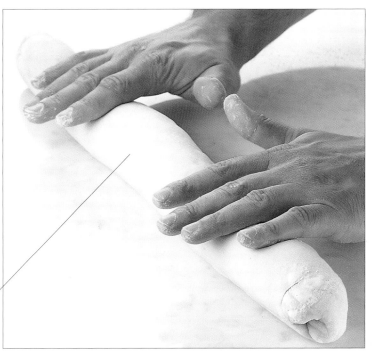

SHAPING A BAGUETTE

TO MAKE A BAGUETTE, shape the dough as for a long loaf following steps 1–4. With your hands placed at either end of the loaf, continue to gently roll the dough backwards and forwards, moving both hands outwards along the loaf. If the dough resists or tightens, allow it to rest for 5 minutes. Repeat the rolling action until an even thickness and the desired length are achieved.

Roll the dough while moving your hands outwards along the loaf

SHAPING DOUGH FOR A LOAF TIN

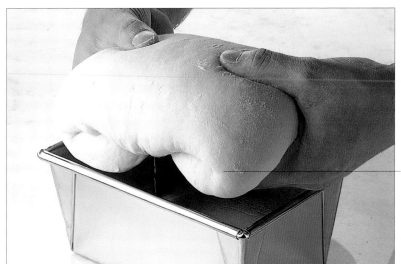

Shape the dough as for a long loaf up to step 3, opposite. Place the dough seam-side down on the work surface. Use the straightened fingers of both hands to gently roll the dough backwards and forwards. Continue until the dough is the same length as the tin and is an even thickness. Lift the dough off the work surface. Tuck under the ends and place the dough into the prepared tin, seam-side down.

Fold the dough to fit the length of the tin

SHAPING A ROUND LOAF

1 Gently press your fingers into the base of the rounded dough (*see page 51*) while holding it with both hands as you would the steering wheel of a car. Rotate the dough between your cupped hands. As the dough is turned, exert light pressure with the tips of your fingers, while at the same time tucking the sides of the dough under what will become the base of the loaf.

2 When the dough becomes smooth and rounded, place the base of the loaf face down on a lightly floured work surface. Cup both hands around the dough and rotate it continuously in a steady, clockwise motion (*see Chafing, page 51*) until a smooth, evenly shaped round is formed. Turn the dough over so that the base is now facing upwards and pinch the seam, or "key", together. Place the loaf "key"-side down on a baking sheet.

Shaping an Oval Loaf

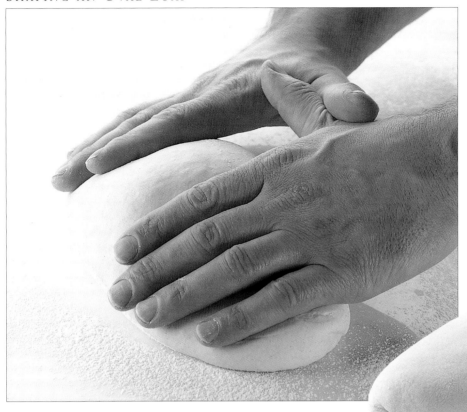

SHAPE THE DOUGH into a round loaf following the directions given opposite. Place the palms of your hands on either side of the round and gently roll the dough backwards and forwards, keeping your hands in the same position. Continue to roll the dough until the ends become slightly tapered and the desired shape is achieved.

FINISHED SHAPE

Round Rolls

TO SHAPE ROUND ROLLS, divide the dough into pieces, each the size of a small lemon. Press down on the pieces to expel any air bubbles. Cup your palm over each piece and roll it over the work surface until it forms a smooth, round ball.

Knotted Rolls

TO SHAPE KNOTTED ROLLS, divide the dough into pieces, each the size of a small lemon. Use the palm of your hand to roll each piece on the work surface to form a rope, 30cm (12in) long and 1cm (½in) thick. Tie each rope into a loose knot.

Twisted Rolls

TO SHAPE TWISTED ROLLS, divide the dough into pieces, each the size of a small lemon. Use the palm of your hand to roll each piece on the work surface to form a rope, 30cm (12in) long and 1cm (½in) thick. Braid two of the ropes together.

SHAPING A COURONNE

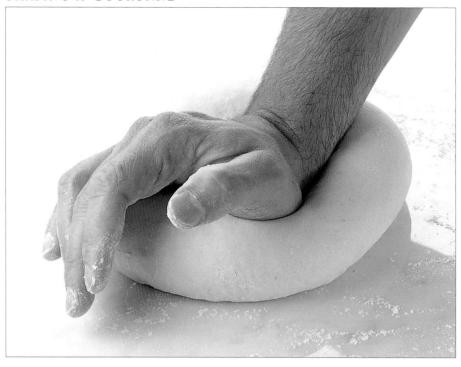

1 Shape the dough into a round (*see page 54*), then flatten the top of the dough with the palm of your hand. Make a hole in the centre of the dough. Place the heel of your hand in the centre of the dough and press right down to the work surface.

Keep your fingers straightened and apply pressure evenly

2 Using both hands, lightly push out the dough with straightened fingers and run them around the inside edge of the hole. Apply pressure evenly to stretch the hole to 15cm (6in) across.

FINISHED SHAPE

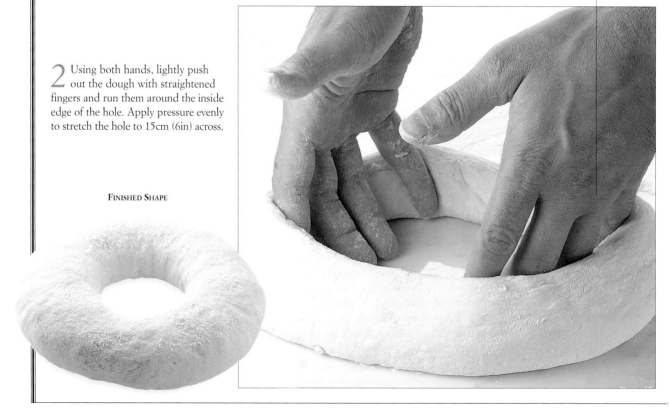

PLAITING

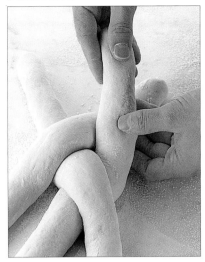

1 Divide the dough into three pieces and roll each one into a 40cm (16in) long rope. Line up the ropes at right angles to the edge of the work surface. Start from the centre of the ropes and plait towards yourself, working from left to right.

2 Continue plaiting the ropes until you reach the end. Press the ends together with your fingers and tuck them neatly under the bottom of the plait. Turn the shaped dough around so that the unplaited end is now facing you.

3 Again, working from the centre, plait the ropes from left to right until you reach the end. Press the ends together and tuck them neatly under the bottom of the plait to finish. Place the completed plait on a baking sheet.

PROVING

PROVING IS REFERRED TO as the final rise. Shaped dough is left to rise until doubled in size (unless otherwise specified in the recipe) on a prepared baking sheet or in a tin just before baking. Proving is best done in a warm, draught-free place. In an exceptionally cold kitchen, a low oven or one heated with just the pilot light is a good option. Preheat the oven for baking halfway through the proving time; remove the bread while the oven preheats.

Avoid over-proving by testing for doneness; press on the dough lightly with your fingertip. The shaped dough is ready to bake when it feels spongy rather than firm and the indentation made with your fingertip springs back slowly. It is best to put bread in the oven a little early (*see page 163*). Do not let shaped dough spread or deflate: over-proving can cause the dough to collapse when touched or slashed, or when it is placed in a hot oven.

UNPROVEN DOUGH

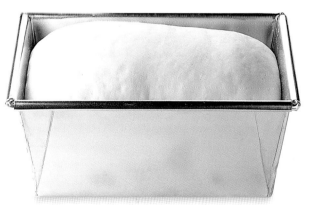

PROVEN DOUGH

GLAZING

ADDING THE FINISHING TOUCHES to a bread is usually done after proving. Glazes can affect the baked taste and texture of the crust as well as the appearance. When a glaze is applied, either before or after baking, depends on the glaze and the effect desired. Some glazes can be brushed on both before and after baking. When applying a glaze before baking be careful not to "glue" the loaf to the rim of the loaf tin or the baking tray. This will not only make it difficult to remove the loaf from the tin, but can prevent the loaf from expanding fully in the oven.

PREPARING AN EGG WASH

1 A basic egg wash will give a shiny, golden look to the crust. It can also be used as an "adhesive" to be applied before any of the toppings described on pages 60–61. To prepare, beat together 1 egg and 1 tablespoon of water, or milk, and a pinch of salt.

Place the shaped dough on a baking sheet, prepared as directed in the recipe, before applying the glaze

2 Gently apply the egg wash to the shaped and proved dough using a clean, soft pastry brush, before baking. For an extra golden sheen, allow the first egg-glaze coating to dry, then apply a second layer of glaze immediately before baking.

Use a clean, soft pastry brush to apply the glaze

Types of Glaze – Before and After Baking

Egg Wash
For a shiny, golden-brown crust, brush the dough with the egg wash (see opposite) before baking.

Milk
For a golden crust, brush the dough with milk before baking. For a slightly sweeter glaze, dissolve a little sugar in warm milk.

Salted Water
For both a light shine and a crisp baked crust, brush the dough with lightly salted water immediately before baking.

Honey
For a soft, sweet, sticky crust, brush a baked, still-warm bread with runny honey. Alternatively, try molasses or corn syrup.

Olive Oil
For both a subtle olive flavour and extra shiny finish, brush the dough immediately before and again after baking with olive oil.

Cornstarch
For a chewy crust, brush the dough with a mixture of cornstarch and water that has been cooked until translucent and then cooled.

Soya Powder and Water
Make a vegan version of egg wash by using a mixture of soya powder and water.

Glazing After Baking

Transfer the loaf or rolls to a wire cooling rack, then apply the prepared glaze, using a soft pastry brush, while the bread is still warm. Glazes are applied after baking to add flavour to the bread and to soften the texture of the crust.

TOPPING

OPPINGS OFFER MANY WAYS to finish a bread before baking. If a flavouring has been used to make the dough, then the loaf may be topped with the same ingredient, providing a clue to the hidden flavour inside. Toppings can also be used to complement a bread or simply to add a decorative touch. Toppings can be applied at different times: before proving, the dough can be rolled in the topping; after proving, it must be handled more gently so it is best to sprinkle the topping over it or use a sieve to create a light dusting.

METHODS OF TOPPING

BEFORE PROVING

SPRINKLE SEEDS or other fine toppings on to a work surface. Gently press the shaped dough into the topping before placing it on a prepared baking sheet to prove.

AFTER PROVING

SPRINKLE COARSE TOPPINGS like chopped nuts or grated cheese over the glazed dough (*see page 58*) after the proving stage or immediately before baking.

BEFORE AND AFTER

USE A FINE MESH SIEVE to lightly dust the shaped dough with flour before and again after proving. This will give the bread's baked crust a dusty, golden finish.

TYPES OF TOPPING – BEFORE AND AFTER BAKING

CRACKED WHEAT
For a crunchy crust, gently press the shaped dough into a bowl of the cracked wheat before placing on a baking sheet to prove.

BRAN FLAKES
To add texture and fibre, glaze the shaped dough with an egg wash (see page 58) and sprinkle bran flakes over the top after proving.

ROLLED OATS
To decorate, glaze the shaped dough with an egg wash (see page 58) and sprinkle the top with rolled oats after proving.

WHITE FLOUR
To create a dusty, golden finish, sift a light dusting of flour over the shaped dough both before proving and before baking.

GRANULATED SUGAR
For a sweet, crackly crust, glaze the shaped dough with an egg wash (see page 58) and sift sugar lightly over it after proving.

PAPRIKA
For both added spice and colour, sprinkle the shaped dough with paprika, or any other ground spice that you choose, after proving.

COARSE SALT
For a salty, crispy crust, glaze the shaped dough with an egg wash (see page 58) and sprinkle coarse salt over the top after proving.

GRATED CHEESE
For a tangy and chewy crust, glaze the shaped dough with an egg wash (see page 58) and sprinkle grated cheese over the top after proving.

FINE CORNMEAL
For colour and a crisp texture, glaze the shaped dough with water only (see page 58) and sprinkle fine cornmeal over the top after proving.

POPPY SEEDS
For a crunchy texture, glaze the shaped dough with an egg wash (see page 58) and sprinkle poppy seeds over the top after proving.

PUMPKIN SEEDS
Arrange pumpkin seeds over the top for a flavourful decoration. Gently press them into the shaped dough before proving.

FRESH HERBS
Use fresh herbs, such as rosemary and thyme, to add flavour and colour. Press them into the shaped dough after proving.

PREPARING FOR BAKING

SLASHING A LOAF before baking has both a functional and a decorative purpose. Cuts made through the surface of the loaf allow the bread to rise and expand as it bakes without tearing or cracking along the sides or bottom. The deeper the slashes, the more the bread will open when baked, giving the baked loaf a maximum area of crust. It is best to cut the slashes using an extremely sharp blade and firm, decisive strokes. If you hesitate as you slash, the dough will stick to the blade, and tear. Steam applied to the oven before or during baking produces a moist heat that helps to create a glazed, crisp crust on the loaf.

SLASHING THE LOAF

USING A BLADE

A RAZOR-SHARP BLADE is the best tool for making clean, perfect slashes. It is worth investing in a scalpel that allows you to safely hold the blade. Use firm, decisive strokes to make the slashes clean and crisp. Keep the slashes equal in depth and length.

SLASHING A TIN LOAF

A LONG SLASH, about 1cm (½in) deep, will allow a tin loaf to rise and open evenly when baked, without breaking open at the sides. With a firm, steady hand plunge the blade into the surface of the loaf and draw it quickly along the length of the loaf.

USING SCISSORS

SHARP SCISSORS are a helpful and effective tool for making decorative slashes. Hold a pair of scissors almost horizontally to cut a *Baguette* into the *Pain d'Epi* variation. Cut about three-quarters of the way through the dough, leaving about 5cm (2in) between each cut. Gently place the flaps to alternate sides.

QUICK SNIPS with a pair of sharp scissors produce a rough, sculptural cut. This is an effective alternative to using a scalpel.

APPLYING STEAM TO THE OVEN

STEAM PLAYS AN IMPORTANT ROLE in many bread recipes, especially those that require a crisp, crusty exterior. It is introduced into the oven before and sometimes during baking. The moisture in the air surrounding the bread in the oven affects both its texture and appearance. Moisture helps to soften the crust during the initial stages of baking. This allows the dough to rise fully, and a thin, crisp outer crust to form. Moisture also helps to caramelize the natural sugars in the bread, resulting in a rich, golden brown crust.

USING A SPRAYER

APPLY STEAM WITH A WATER SPRAYER after placing the loaf in the preheated oven. Mist the oven walls eight to ten times, then repeat the process after 2 minutes and again after 2 minutes more. Shut the door rapidly each time to minimize any heat loss from the oven. Be careful to spray only the sides of the oven, avoiding the oven light, electric heating coils, and oven fan.

USING ICE CUBES

APPLY STEAM BY PLACING A WIDE DISH of ice cubes on the bottom rack or floor of the oven while the oven preheats. Place the loaf in the oven before the ice cubes have completely melted. When the ice cubes have melted, carefully remove the dish from the oven. This should occur within the first 15–20 minutes of the bread's baking time.

USING CERAMIC TILES

LINE THE BOTTOM RACK of the oven with unglazed ceramic tiles, leaving 5cm (2in) of air space around the tiles and the oven wall to allow for air circulation. The tiles will produce a steady, radiating heat and help to retain a maximum amount of moisture in the oven. When tiles are used in combination with the applied steam methods and the bread is baked directly on the tiled surface, it will form the crispest crust of the three methods.

BAKING

B AKING IS THE CULMINATION of the breadmaking process, when all of your hard work and patience are rewarded. For a successful loaf follow these simple guidelines: use a good thermometer to regulate the temperature of the oven; preheat to the correct temperature before placing the bread in the oven to bake; make a note of the exact baking time before beginning; and always use a kitchen timer to keep track of the time. An important key to proficient baking lies in knowing your oven and being able to control its temperature closely – each oven is slightly different and has its own peculiarities.

BAKING STAGES

1 When the bread is placed in the hot oven, the heat turns the moisture in the dough to steam, causing the loaf to rise rapidly in the first 20 minutes of baking. The heat then penetrates the bread, killing the active yeast cells and allowing the exterior crust to form.

GETTING TO KNOW YOUR OVEN
Since each oven is different it is difficult to establish hard and fast rules for breadmaking, such as oven shelf position. The only solution is increased familiarity with your oven. Using an oven thermometer before and during baking allows you to observe any variations in temperature and to make adjustments. If you find that you have "hot spots" (uneven heat), in your oven it is important to turn the bread half-way through baking.

2 As the exterior crust forms, the natural sugars in the dough caramelize, creating a golden brown colour. The baking time is specified in each recipe. High humidity, however, can sometimes extend the required baking time and needs to be taken into consideration on the day of baking.

The dough's natural sugars caramelize to give a golden crust

TESTING FOR DONENESS

UNDERCOOKING BREAD is a common mistake of the novice baker. Bread is indigestible when it has been undercooked so it is important to test for doneness. A well-baked bread should be golden brown, not too pale or too dark in colour. The texture and feel of the bread should be firm to the touch without seeming hard. The best test, however, is to listen to the sound of the baked loaf when it is tapped on the underside. It should sound slightly hollow when it has been properly cooked.

COOLING

IT IS IMPORTANT to allow a freshly baked loaf to cool on a wire rack. As the loaf cools, steam from the middle works its way towards the crust, causing it to soften. Cooling baked bread on a wire rack prevents the bottom crust from becoming damp and soggy.

SLICING

WHEN SLICING BREAD use a sharp, serrated bread knife and a clean bread board. Breads should be left to cool slightly before slicing. Use a steady, sawing motion across the top of the bread to prevent the weight of the knife from crushing the loaf or tearing the crust.

USING A BREAD MACHINE

THE MANUFACTURER'S INSTRUCTION MANUAL is an invaluable resource for getting the best results from your machine. A bread machine will mix, knead, rise and bake a loaf. Machine models vary in the shape and the size of loaf they make as well as in how they operate. Some machines have programmable cycles for making different kinds of bread dough, others offer fewer alternatives. A recipe booklet comes with most models. Master a few of these recipes to familiarize yourself with the way your machine works, its possibilities and its limitations. Use the experience to adapt the recipes in this book following the general guidelines given here.

1 Add the ingredients to the baking cylinder in the order suggested in the instruction manual. This will vary depending on the machine model you have. The manufacturer's instructions will tell you what type of yeast to use. The best results are achieved with a yeast made for bread machines; easy-blend yeast also works. Place the baking cylinder inside the machine, select a setting on the control panel, according to the manual, and press start.

HANDY TIPS

• *Pay attention to the order in which the ingredients are added to the machine; it does make a difference.*

• *Keep the lid open to watch the mixing and kneading cycles, but make sure that the lid is shut during rising and baking.*

• *Use the handle of a wooden spoon to remove the kneading paddle from the bottom of the hot, baked loaf.*

2 Check the dough about 10 minutes into the kneading cycle. It should be smooth and soft at this stage (*right*). If it is too soft, add extra flour 1 tablespoon at a time. If it is stiff, add extra water 1 tablespoon at a time. Ingredients like nuts and dried fruits should be added in the last few minutes of the kneading cycle.

3 When the bread is baked, remove it immediately from the machine and the baking cylinder to prevent a soggy crust. Leave it to cool on to a wire rack.

USING THE RECIPES IN THIS BOOK

Depending on the capacity of your machine, many of the basic bread recipes, excluding those using a starter (*see pages 84–93*), may be mixed and kneaded in a bread machine. Most machines call for using bread machine yeast, or easy-blend yeast, which means eliminating the sponge method from the recipe instructions. Add the ingredients in the order suggested in the manufacturer's manual and select the correct machine settings. Remove the dough from the machine after the rising period, and before the proving (final rise) and baking cycles begin. Instead shape, prove, and bake according to the recipe.

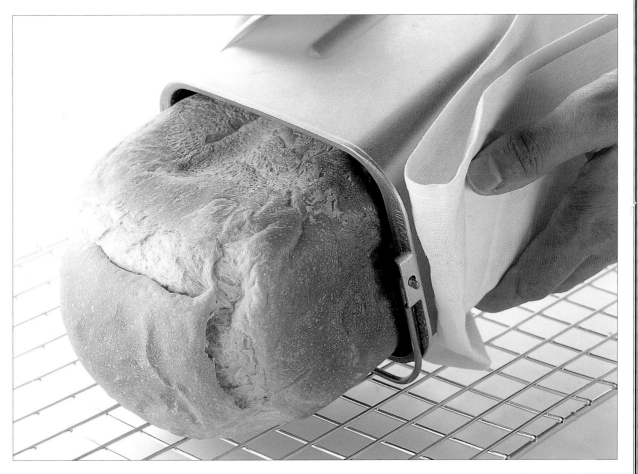

STORING & FREEZING

SOME BREADS ARE BEST EATEN on the day of baking, but most home-baked breads keep for anything from a couple of days to up to a week. As a general rule, storage time depends on the ingredients used and the size of the loaf. A large, thick loaf will usually dry out more slowly than a small, thin one. Breads enriched with oil,

butter, or eggs (*see pages 110–125*) tend to last longer than plain breads, and those made with a starter (*see pages 84–93*) also have a longer shelf life. Bread dough can easily be frozen, either before or after rising, which allows greater flexibility in the breadmaking schedule. Baked bread also freezes and defrosts successfully.

STORING BAKED BREAD

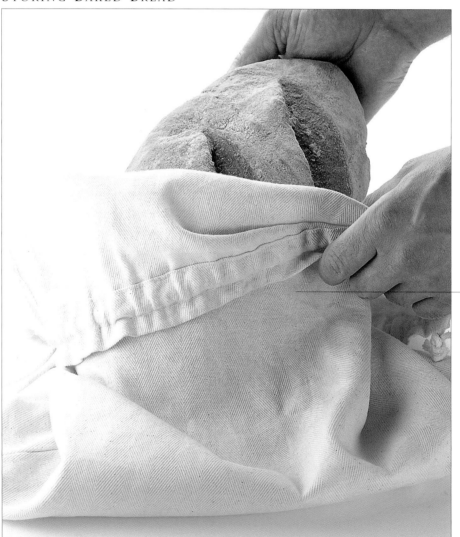

A clean, dry cloth bag is the best place to store bread after it has cooled

ONLY STORE BREAD after it has cooled. Any residual warmth left in the bread will continue to give off steam, which will condense inside the wrapping or container, resulting in a stale texture and rapid moulding. When the bread has cooled completely, wrap in a clean, dry cloth or bread bag and store at room temperature. If stored like this bread will remain fresh for 3–4 days. Never refrigerate bread because this dehydrates it and accelerates staling.

REFRESHING STALE BREAD
Spray the bread lightly with tap water, wrap in foil, and warm in an oven, 200°C/400°F/gas 6, for 10 minutes. Microwave ovens are not recommended for refreshing stale bread; microwaving tends to dry out and harden bread.

FREEZING UNRISEN DOUGH

FREEZING SHAPED DOUGH

WHEN AVAILABLE TIME is limited dough can be frozen before rising and shaping. Mix and knead the dough as directed in the recipe. Brush the inside of a plastic freezer bag with oil and place the unrisen dough inside. Expel any air, leaving just enough space for the dough to rise slightly as it freezes. To thaw, place the dough in the refrigerator for 12–24 hours, until it doubles in size. Remove from the refrigerator and bring the dough to room temperature. Shape, prove, and bake as directed.

WHEN IT IS CONVENIENT the dough can be frozen after shaping. Place the shaped dough on a baking sheet and cover tightly with clingfilm. Then place the baking sheet in the freezer and leave just until the dough becomes firm. Store the shaped dough in a plastic freezer bag. To thaw, remove the dough from the bag and place it in the refrigerator for 12–24 hours, until it has doubled in size. Remove from the refrigerator and leave at room temperature for 20 minutes. Bake as directed.

FREEZING BAKED BREAD

FRESHLY BAKED BREAD can be frozen successfully after it has cooled completely. Wrap the bread in heavy-duty foil, then place it in a plastic freezer bag; expel all the air before sealing. The bread will keep for up to 3 months.

Use heavy-duty foil to wrap bread before freezing

DEFROSTING BREAD

Defrost bread slowly at a cool room temperature for three to six hours, or in the refrigerator for eight to ten hours. Bread defrosted slowly will retain its freshness for longer. Defrost bread in its wrapping to prevent it from drying out. Crispen breads with a thick crust in a low oven before serving. To defrost bread more quickly place the wrapped loaf in a preheated oven, 200°C/400°F/gas 6, for about 45 minutes.

RECIPES

OVER 100 BREADS CAN BE CREATED USING THIS RECIPE SECTION. EACH ONE IS A VARIATION ON A VERY SIMPLE THEME: FLOUR, WATER, LEAVENING, AND TIME. BEGIN WITH THE BASIC AND STARTER BREAD RECIPES, WHICH UTILIZE METHODS ILLUSTRATED IN THE BASIC TECHNIQUES. FLAVOURED BREADS PROVIDE AN EXTRA TASTE DIMENSION, WHILE ENRICHED BREADS TRANSFORM BASIC BREAD DOUGH WITH THE ADDITIONS OF OIL, BUTTER, AND EGGS. QUICK, FLAT, AND FESTIVE BREADS OFFER OTHER DELICIOUS POSSIBILITIES FROM AROUND THE WORLD.

BASIC BREADS

THE RECIPES IN THIS CHAPTER require no advanced skills, only your hands, your attention, and your time. They represent the backbone of the book utilizing the skills covered in the Basic Techniques section (*see pages 38–69*). Read this section first and you will be able to tackle all of the basic bread recipes with ease and confidence. These simple breads give the novice baker the opportunity to experiment, to observe the transformation of the ingredients into bread, and to gain valuable experience. Later in the recipe section other elements, such as starters, flavourings, and enrichments are added to the basic ingredients of flour, water, and yeast. These additions introduce the baker to new techniques and skills illustrated with the recipes.

PAIN ORDINAIRE
PLAIN OR BASIC WHITE BREAD

Treat this recipe as a blueprint for the basic method of breadmaking. A wide variety of breads can be created using this simple dough recipe. For a more rustic flavour, substitute 125g (4oz) of wholemeal, rye, or barley flour for the same amount of strong white flour. For an extra-tender crumb, substitute 175ml (6fl oz) of the water for the same amount of yogurt or buttermilk and add it to the well in step 3.

INGREDIENTS
2 tsp dried yeast

350ml (12fl oz) water

500g (1lb) strong white flour

1½ tsp salt

1 Sprinkle the yeast into 100ml (3½fl oz) of the water in a bowl. Leave for 5 minutes; stir to dissolve. Mix the flour and salt together in a large bowl. Make a well in the centre and pour in the yeasted water.

2 Use a wooden spoon to draw enough of the flour into the yeasted water to form a soft paste. Cover the bowl with a tea towel and leave the paste to "sponge" until frothy, loose, and slightly expanded, about 20 minutes.

3 Pour the remaining water, holding back about half, into the centre of the well. Mix in the flour from the sides of the well. Stir in the reserved water, as needed, to form a firm, moist dough.

4 Turn the dough out on to a lightly floured work surface. Knead until smooth, shiny, and elastic, about 10 minutes.

5 Put the dough in a clean bowl and cover with a tea towel. Leave to rise until doubled in size, about 1½–2 hours.

6 Knock back, then leave to rest for 10 minutes. Shape the dough into a long loaf (*see pages 52–53*), about 35cm (14in) in length. Place the shaped loaf on a floured baking sheet and cover with a tea towel. Prove until doubled in size, about 45 minutes.

7 Cut five diagonal slashes (*see page 62*), each about 5mm (¼in) deep, across the top of the loaf. Bake in the preheated oven for 45 minutes until golden brown and hollow-sounding when tapped underneath. Leave the baked bread to cool on a wire rack.

To begin
Sponge method
Time: 20 minutes
(*see page 44*)

Rising
1½–2 hours
(*see pages 50–51*)

Proving
45 minutes
(*see page 57*)

Oven temperature
220°C/425°F/gas 7

Baking
45 minutes
Steam optional
(*see page 63*)

Yield
1 loaf

Yeast alternative
15g (½oz) fresh yeast
(*see page 41*)

CLASSIC PAIN ORDINAIRE

SHAPING A COTTAGE LOAF

Divide the dough into two-thirds and a third. Shape each piece into a round loaf (see pages 54–55). Place the small loaf on top of the large loaf. Plunge two fingers into the centres of the stacked loaves to join them together.

VARIATIONS

Cottage Loaf

• Make one quantity Pain Ordinaire dough up to step 6.

• Shape the bread dough into a cottage loaf shape (*see left*).

• Place on a floured baking sheet and cover with a tea towel. Prove until doubled in size, about 45 minutes. Preheat the oven to 220°C/425°F/gas 7. Sift over a dusting of flour.

• Bake for 45 minutes, as directed in step 7. Cool on a wire rack.

Petits Pains (Bread Rolls)

• Make one quantity Pain Ordinaire dough up to step 6.

• Divide the bread dough into eight pieces and shape into smooth, round rolls (*see page 55*).

• Place on a floured baking sheet and cover with a tea towel. Prove until doubled in size, about 30 minutes. Preheat the oven to 220°C/425°F/gas 7.

• Sift over a light dusting of flour. Use a pair of scissors to snip an "X" in the centre of each roll (*see page 62*).

• Bake for 25 minutes until hollow-sounding when tapped underneath. Leave to cool on a wire rack.

Granary Tin Loaf

• Make one quantity Pain Ordinaire dough up to step 6, replacing the strong white flour with the same amount of granary flour in step 1.

• Grease a 500g (1lb) loaf tin with oil. Shape the dough for a loaf tin (*see page 53*) and place the dough in the tin, seam-side down.

• Cover with a tea towel and prove until the dough is 1cm (½in) below the top of the tin, about 30 minutes.

• If desired, cut a lengthways slash (*see page 62*) for a split tin loaf. Leave the dough to rise further until it is 1cm (½in) above the top of the tin, about 15 minutes. Preheat the oven to 220°C/425°F/gas 7.

• Brush the top with water and bake for 20 minutes. Reduce the oven to 200°C/400°F/gas 6 and bake for a further 15–20 minutes, until hollow-sounding when tapped. Turn out on to a wire rack and leave to cool.

— HANDY TIPS —

• *Use tepid water to dissolve the yeast (see page 41). Tepid water should be comfortable to the touch, not too hot, but not too cool.*

• *It is important that the dough is soft and not too dry before it is kneaded. Add more water 1 tablespoon at a time, as needed, to achieve a consistency indicated in the recipe.*

• *When kneading the dough use extra flour sparingly. Work the dough slowly and firmly; it will gradually become more elastic and easier to knead.*

USING A BREAD MACHINE

Use the dough setting (see pages 66–67). Remove the dough after rising and follow steps 6 and 7.

COTTAGE LOAF

GRANARY TIN LOAF

PETITS PAINS

COUNTRY OATMEAL BREAD

Sometimes called Monastery bread, this coarse, crunchy British bread originated in northern England. It is best eaten for breakfast or afternoon tea, thickly spread with yellow, salted butter and fragrant, creamy honey, or try it with a chunk of Cheddar cheese and a mug of ale.

USING A BREAD MACHINE

Use the dough setting (see pages 66–67). Remove the dough after rising and follow steps 5 and 6.

INGREDIENTS

2 tsp dried yeast

350ml (12fl oz) water

250g (8oz) wholemeal flour

125g (4oz) strong white flour

125g (4oz) medium oatmeal

1½ tsp salt

1 tsp runny honey

rolled oats, for topping

1 Sprinkle the yeast into 100ml (3½fl oz) of the water in a bowl. Leave for 5 minutes; stir to dissolve. Mix the flours, oatmeal, and salt together in a large bowl. Make a well in the centre and pour in the yeasted water and runny honey.

2 Pour the remaining water, holding back about half, into the well. Mix in the flour, then stir in the reserved water, as needed, to form a stiff, sticky dough.

3 Turn the dough out on to a work surface lightly sprinkled with oatmeal. Knead until smooth and elastic, about 10 minutes.

4 Put the dough in a clean bowl and cover with a tea towel. Leave to rise until doubled in size, about 1½–2 hours.

5 Knock back, then leave to rest for 10 minutes. Grease a 500g (1lb) loaf tin. Shape the dough for a loaf tin (*see page 53*). Place the dough in the tin, seam-side down. Cover with a tea towel and prove until doubled in size, about 1 hour.

6 Brush the loaf lightly with water and sprinkle with rolled oats over the top. Bake in the preheated oven for 1 hour until golden brown and hollow-sounding when tapped underneath. Turn out of the tin and leave to cool on a wire rack.

VARIATIONS

Barley Bread

• Make one quantity Country Oatmeal Bread dough. Replace the flours with 250g (8oz) strong white flour, 125g (4oz) barley flour, and 125g (4oz) wholemeal flour. Follow the recipe up to step 6. Preheat the oven to 200°C/400°F/gas 6.

• Brush the loaf lightly with water and sprinkle with barley flakes instead of the rolled oats in step 6.

• Bake for 1 hour until golden brown and hollow-sounding when tapped underneath. Turn out and leave to cool on a wire rack.

Oatmeal Rolls

• Make one quantity Country Oatmeal Bread dough up to step 4.

• Divide the dough into 16 equal pieces and shape into smooth, round rolls (*see page 55*). Place the rolls on two greased baking sheets. Cover with a tea towel and prove until doubled in size, about 30–45 minutes. Preheat the oven to 200°C/400°F/gas 6.

• Brush the rolls lightly with water and sprinkle with rolled oats.

• Bake for 20–30 minutes until golden and hollow-sounding when tapped underneath. Leave to cool on a wire rack.

Rising
1½–2 hours
(*see pages 50–51*)

Proving
1 hour
(*see page 57*)

Oven temperature
200°C/400°F/gas 6

Baking
1 hour
Steam optional
(*see page 63*)

Yield
1 loaf

Yeast alternative
15g (½oz)
fresh yeast
(*see page 41*)

DAKTYLA
GREEK VILLAGE BREAD

This sesame seed-coated bread is traditionally made with "yellow" or "country" flour, a blend of white and wholemeal flour mixed with finely ground cornmeal. Alternatively, it can be made just with strong white flour. In Greece, the bread is commonly known as Daktyla, meaning "fingers", because it is broken into fingers of bread to eat.

USING A BREAD MACHINE
Use the dough setting (see pages 66–67). Remove the dough after rising and follow steps 6 and 7.

INGREDIENTS
2 tsp dried yeast

350ml (12fl oz) water

350g (12oz) strong white flour

75g (2½oz) wholemeal flour

75g (2½oz) fine cornmeal

1 tsp salt

1 tbsp olive oil

1 tbsp runny honey

1 tbsp milk, plus extra to glaze

sesame seeds, to decorate

1 Sprinkle the yeast into 100ml (3½fl oz) of the water in a bowl. Leave for 5 minutes; stir to dissolve. Mix the flours, cornmeal, and salt together thoroughly in a large bowl. Make a well in the centre and pour in the yeasted water.

2 Use a wooden spoon to draw enough of the flour into the yeasted water to form a soft paste. Cover the bowl with a tea towel, then leave to "sponge" until frothy and risen, 20 minutes. Add the oil, honey, and milk to the sponge.

3 Pour the remaining water, holding back about half, into the well. Mix in the flour. Stir in the reserved liquid, as needed, to form a firm, moist dough.

4 Turn the dough out on to a lightly floured work surface. Knead until smooth, shiny, and elastic, about 10 minutes.

5 Put the dough in a clean bowl and cover with a tea towel. Leave to rise until doubled in size, about 1½ hours.

6 Knock back, leave to rest for 10 minutes. Divide the dough into six pieces. Shape each piece into an oblong, then arrange in a row, just touching, on a floured baking sheet. Cover with a tea towel and prove until doubled in size, about 1 hour.

7 Brush the top of the loaf with milk and sprinkle with the sesame seeds. Bake in the preheated oven for 45 minutes until hollow-sounding when tapped underneath. Leave to cool on a wire rack.

To begin
Sponge method
Time: 20 minutes
(see page 44)

Rising
1½ hours
(see pages 50–51)

Proving
1 hour
(see page 57)

Oven temperature
220°C/425°F/gas 7

Baking
45 minutes
Steam optional
(see page 63)

Yield
1 loaf

Yeast alternative
15g (½oz)
fresh yeast
(see page 41)

VICTORIAN MILK BREAD

This is a bread with a soft crust and crumb, which keeps well and makes crisp, nutty toast. It is a very good dough for making a decorative plait (see page 57).

USING A BREAD MACHINE

Use the dough setting (see pages 66–67). Remove the dough after rising and follow steps 5 and 6.

INGREDIENTS

2 tsp dried yeast

1 tsp granulated sugar

350ml (12fl oz) tepid milk

500g (1lb) strong white flour

1½ tsp salt

egg glaze, made with 1 egg and 1 tbsp milk (see page 58)

1 Sprinkle the yeast and sugar into 100ml (3½fl oz) of milk in a bowl. Leave for 5 minutes; stir to dissolve. Stir in half of the remaining milk.

2 Mix the flour and salt together in a large bowl. Make a well in the centre and pour in the yeasted milk. Mix in the flour. Stir in the reserved milk to form a sticky dough.

3 Turn the dough out on to a lightly floured work surface. Knead the dough until smooth and elastic, about 10 minutes.

4 Put the dough in a clean bowl and cover with a tea towel. Leave to rise for 45 minutes.

5 Knock back, cover, and leave the dough to rise again until doubled in size, about 45 minutes. Grease a 500g (1lb) loaf tin. Shape the dough into an S-shape to fit in a loaf tin (*see right*). Cover with a tea towel, then prove until the dough is 2.5cm (1in) above the top of the tin, about 1 hour.

6 Brush the top of the loaf with the egg glaze. Bake in the preheated oven for 45 minutes until golden and hollow-sounding when tapped underneath. Turn out on to a wire rack and leave to cool.

VARIATION
Bloomer
(see page 16 for illustration)
• Make one quantity Victorian Milk Bread dough, replacing half the milk with water, up to step 4.
• Leave to rise for 2 hours. Knock back and leave to rest for 5 minutes.
• Shape into a long loaf, about 25cm (10in) in length and 12.5cm (5in) wide (*see pages 52–53*). Prove as directed, about 1 hour.
• Cut five deep slashes across the top of the loaf (*see page 62*). Preheat the oven to 220°C/425°F/gas 7.
• Sift over a fine layer of flour. Bake as directed in step 6.

 Rising
1½ hours
(*see pages 50–51*)

 Proving
1 hour
(*see page 57*)

 Oven temperature
200°C/400°F/gas 6

 Baking
45 minutes

 Yield
1 loaf

 Yeast alternative
15g (½oz)
fresh yeast
(*see page 41*)

SHAPING THE DOUGH

Shape the dough into a long loaf (see pages 52–53), about 40cm (16in) in length and 7.5cm (3¼in) wide. Turn the shaped dough over at each end to form an S-shape. Place the dough in the greased loaf tin. Continue as directed in step 5.

SCOTS BAPS

Scots Baps are best eaten warm, straight from the oven. They are a special treat at breakfast when filled with grilled bacon rashers and a fried egg. The mixture of milk and water gives the rolls a tender crumb and the extra dusting of flour gives them a soft crust.

USING A BREAD MACHINE

Use the dough setting (see pages 66–67). Remove the dough after rising and follow steps 5–8.

INGREDIENTS

175ml (6fl oz) tepid milk

175ml (6fl oz) water

2 tsp dried yeast

1 tsp granulated sugar

500g (1lb) strong white flour

1½ tsp salt

1 tbsp milk, to glaze

1 Combine the milk and water in a liquid measuring jug. Sprinkle the yeast and sugar into 100ml (3½fl oz) of the milk and water mixture in a separate bowl. Leave for 5 minutes; stir to dissolve. Stir in half of the remaining milk and water mixture.

2 Mix the flour and salt together in a large bowl. Make a well in the centre and pour in the yeasted milk and water. Mix in the flour. Stir in the reserved milk and water, as needed, to form a sticky dough.

3 Turn the dough out on to a lightly floured work surface. Knead the dough until smooth and elastic, about 10 minutes.

4 Put the dough in a clean bowl and cover with a tea towel. Leave to rise until doubled in size, about 1 hour.

5 Knock back, leave to rest for 10 minutes. Divide into eight pieces. Shape each one into a flat oval, about 1cm (½in) thick. Put on a floured baking sheet. Brush with milk and sift over a heavy dusting of flour.

6 Leave to prove, uncovered, until doubled in size, 30–45 minutes.

7 Sift a heavy dusting of flour again over each bap. Use your thumb to make an impression in the centre of each bap, about 1cm (½in) deep.

8 Bake in the preheated oven for 15–20 minutes until risen and pale golden. Cover with a tea towel and leave to cool on a wire rack.

VARIATION
Kentish Huffkins

- Make one quantity Scots Baps dough up to step 4.
- Divide the dough into 12 equal pieces. Shape each piece of dough into a round ball (*see page 55*). Place on a floured baking sheet.
- Use a floured finger to form a deep indentation in the centre of each roll. Prove until doubled in size, 30–45 minutes. Preheat the oven to 200°C/400°F/gas 6.
- Bake as directed in step 8. Leave to cool on a wire rack. Fill the indent with jam and cream to serve.

 Rising
1 hour
(*see pages 50–51*)

 Proving
30–45 minutes
(*see page 57*)

 Oven temperature
200°C/400°F/gas 6

 Baking
15–20 minutes

 Yield
8 baps

 Yeast alternative
15g (½oz)
fresh yeast
(*see page 41*)

BALLYMALOE BROWN BREAD

This no-knead bread revolutionized English women's lives in the 1940s when it was introduced by Doris Grant in her book Your Daily Bread. This improved version was devised by Myrtle Allen, founder of Ballymaloe House hotel and cookery school in County Cork, Ireland.

USING A BREAD MACHINE

This bread may be made entirely in a machine. Follow the manufacturer's instructions (see pages 66–67).

INGREDIENTS

3½ tsp dried yeast

400ml (14fl oz) water

1 tsp black treacle or molasses

500g (1lb) wholemeal flour

2 tsp salt

1 Grease a 500g (1lb) loaf tin and warm it in a preheated oven, 120°C/250°F/gas ½ for 10 minutes.

2 Sprinkle the yeast into 150ml (¼ pint) of the water in a bowl. Leave for 5 minutes; stir to dissolve. Add the treacle or molasses. Leave for a further 10 minutes until frothy. Add the remaining water and stir.

3 Mix the flour and salt together in a large bowl. Make a well in the centre and pour in the yeasted mixture. Stir in the flour from the sides to form a thick batter.

4 Use your hands to mix the batter gently in the bowl for 1 minute until it begins to leave the sides of the bowl clean, and forms into a soft, sticky dough.

5 Place the dough in the prepared tin and cover with a tea towel. Leave to prove until the dough is 1cm (½in) above the top of the tin, about 25–30 minutes.

6 Bake in the preheated oven at 220°C/425°F/gas 7 for 30 minutes, then lower the temperature to 200°C/400°F/gas 6 and bake for a further 15 minutes.

7 Turn the loaf out on to a baking sheet. Return the bread, bottom-side up, to the oven. Bake for a further 10 minutes until golden and hollow-sounding when tapped underneath. Cool on a wire rack.

Proving
25–30 minutes
(*see page 57*)

Oven temperature
220°C/425°F/gas 7

Baking
55 minutes

Yield
1 loaf

Yeast alternative
30g (1oz)
fresh yeast
(*see page 41*)

BROA

PORTUGUESE CORN BREAD

This famous yellow cornmeal bread originated in the Minho province in northern Portugal. It is eaten traditionally with Caldo Verde, Portugal's famous kale and sausage soup. (See page 19 for an illustration of the bread.)

USING A BREAD MACHINE

Use the dough setting (see pages 66–67). Remove the dough after rising and follow steps 5 and 6.

INGREDIENTS

2 tsp dried yeast

150ml (¼ pint) tepid milk

200ml (7fl oz) water

200g (7oz) yellow cornmeal

300g (10oz) strong white flour, sifted

1½ tsp salt

1 tbsp olive oil

1 Sprinkle the yeast into the milk in a bowl. Leave for 5 minutes; stir with a wooden spoon. Add the water to the milk. Mix the cornmeal, flour, and salt in a large bowl. Make a well in the centre and pour in the yeasted liquid and olive oil.

2 Mix in the flour to form a firm and moist, but not sticky, dough that leaves the sides of the bowl.

3 Turn the dough out on to a lightly floured work surface. Knead the dough until smooth and elastic, about 10 minutes.

4 Put the dough in a clean bowl and cover with a tea towel. Leave to rise until doubled in size, about 1½ hours.

5 Knock back, leave to rest for 10 minutes. Shape into a round loaf (*see page 54*). Place on a baking sheet sprinkled with corn-meal and cover with a tea towel. Prove until doubled in size, about 1 hour.

6 Dust the loaf with cornmeal. Bake in the preheated oven for 45 minutes until golden and hollow-sounding when tapped underneath. Leave to cool on a wire rack.

Rising
1½ hours
(*see pages 50–51*)

Proving
1 hour
(*see page 57*)

Oven temperature
200°C/400°F/gas 6

Baking
45 minutes
Steam optional
(*see page 63*)

Yield
1 loaf

Yeast alternative
15g (½oz)
fresh yeast
(*see page 41*)

BAGUETTE

FRENCH STICK

This long, thin loaf with a crisp, golden crust and light, chewy interior is more commonly known in the English-speaking world as a French Stick. It translates literally to "little rod" and, in French, also means a fairy's wand or a conductor's baton.

USING A BREAD MACHINE

Use the dough setting (see pages 66–67). Remove the dough after rising and follow steps 6–8.

BAGUETTE

INGREDIENTS

2½ tsp dried yeast

375ml (13fl oz) water

500g (1lb) strong white flour

1½ tsp salt

1 Sprinkle the yeast into 300ml (½ pint) of the water in a bowl. Leave for 5 minutes; stir to dissolve. Mix the flour and salt in a large bowl. Make a well in the centre and pour in the yeasted water.

2 Use a wooden spoon to draw enough of the flour into the yeasted water to form a soft paste. Cover the bowl with a tea towel then leave to "sponge" until frothy and risen, about 20 minutes.

3 Mix in the flour and add the remaining water as needed, 1 tablespoon at a time, to form a soft, sticky dough.

4 Turn out on to a lightly floured work surface. Knead until soft, smooth and supple, about 10 minutes. Try to avoid adding any extra flour while kneading the dough.

5 Put the dough in a clean bowl and cover with a tea towel. Leave to rise until doubled in size, about 1½ hours.

6 Knock back, re-cover and leave to rise for a further 45 minutes. Knock back again, re-cover and leave to rise until doubled in size, about 45 minutes.

7 Divide the dough into two equal-sized pieces and shape into two baguettes (*see pages 52–53*), each about 30cm (12in) in length. Place on a floured baking sheet or in a floured baguette tray (*see page 37*); cover with a tea towel. Prove until doubled in size, about 50 minutes.

8 Cut several diagonal slashes (*see page 62*) across the top. Bake in the preheated oven for 20–25 minutes until golden and hollow-sounding when tapped underneath. Cool on a wire rack.

VARIATIONS

Pistolets (Split Rolls)
(see page 12 for illustration)

• Make one quantity Baguette dough up to step 7. Divide the dough into eight equal pieces and shape each piece into a smooth ball (*see page 55*).

• Sift a dusting of flour over the dough balls. Use the handle of a wooden spoon to make a deep indentation across the centre of each ball, pressing down through the dough almost to the work surface. Place the split rolls well apart on a floured baking sheet.

• Sift a dusting of flour over each roll to prevent the two halves of the roll from sticking together during proving and baking.

• Cover with a tea towel and leave to prove until doubled in size, about 30 minutes. Preheat the oven to 220°C/425°F/gas 7.

• Bake for 20–25 minutes until golden. Cool on a wire rack.

• This roll shape also works well when made with Pain Ordinaire dough (*see page 72*) and Pain de Campagne dough (*see page 84*).

Pain d'Epi
("Ear of Wheat")

• Make one quantity Baguette dough up to step 7. Divide the dough and shape into two baguettes (*see pages 52–53*) each about 30cm (12in) long. Use sharp scissors to cut the loaves (*see page 62*).

• Place on a floured baking sheet; cover with a tea towel. Prove until doubled in size, about 50 minutes. Preheat the oven to 220°C/425°F/gas 7. Bake for 20–25 minutes. Cool on a wire rack.

To begin
Sponge method
Time: 20 minutes
(*see page 44*)

Rising
3 hours
(*see pages 50–51*)

Proving
50 minutes
(*see page 57*)

Oven temperature
240°C/475°F/gas 9

Baking
20–25 minutes
Steam optional
(*see page 63*)

Yield
2 loaves

Yeast alternative
20g (¾oz)
fresh yeast
(*see page 41*)

PAIN D'EPI

GRISSINI TORINESI
ITALIAN BREADSTICKS

These famous Italian breadsticks are served with an antipasto, or starter. They are easily digested, designed not to curb the diner's appetite for the rest of the meal. Coat them with any spice, herb, or seed you desire: replace the sesame seeds with the topping of your choice, such as coarse sea salt, fresh rosemary, or dried fennel seeds. Sprinkle the topping over the sticks after they have been brushed with the egg glaze and bake as directed in step 6.

USING A BREAD MACHINE
This recipe is not suitable for bread machines.

INGREDIENTS

2 tsp dried yeast

325ml (11fl oz) water

1 tsp malt extract

500g (1lb) strong white flour, sifted

2 tsp salt

3 tbsp olive oil

2 tbsp semolina

egg glaze, made with 1 egg yolk and 1 tbsp water (see page 58)

sesame seeds, for topping

1 Sprinkle the yeast into 125ml (4fl oz) of the water in a bowl. Leave for 5 minutes, then add the malt extract; stir to dissolve. Mix the flour and the salt together in a large bowl. Make a well in the centre and pour in the yeasted liquid and the olive oil.

2 Use a wooden spoon to draw the flour in from the sides. Stir in the remaining water, as needed, to form a firm, sticky dough.

3 Turn the dough out on to a well-floured work surface. Knead the dough until smooth and elastic, about 10 minutes. Cover with a tea towel and leave to rest for 10 minutes. Knead the dough for a further 10 minutes.

4 Shape the dough into a rectangle, 30cm x 20cm (12in x 8in) and 1.5cm (⅝in) thick. Cover with a tea towel; leave to rest for 10 minutes.

5 Lightly oil two baking sheets and sprinkle them with semolina. Cut the dough rectangle lengthways into four equal pieces, then cut each piece lengthways into ten strips. Stretch each strip until it is 25cm (10in) long. Place the strips, about 1cm (½in) apart, on the baking sheets.

6 Brush the strips with the egg glaze and sprinkle with sesame seeds. Bake in the preheated oven for 15–20 minutes. Transfer the sticks on to a wire rack, then leave to cool.

VARIATION
Picos (Spanish Bread Loops)
• Make one quantity Grissini Torinesi dough up to step 4.
• Divide the dough into two equal-sized pieces. Shape each piece into a rectangle, about 20cm x 15cm (8in x 6in). Cover with a tea towel, then leave to rest for 10 minutes. Preheat the oven to 220°C/425°F/gas 7.
• Cut each rectangle lengthways into 16 equal-sized strips, then cut each dough strip in half to make 64 pieces of dough. Tie each strip in a single knot (*see page 55*). Place each knot on a lightly oiled baking sheet. Brush with water and, if desired, sprinkle with coarse sea salt.
• Bake as directed in step 6. Leave to cool on a wire rack.

Oven temperature
200°C/400°F/gas 6

Baking
15–20 minutes
Steam optional
(*see page 63*)

Yield
40 breadsticks

Yeast alternative
15g (½oz)
fresh yeast
(*see page 41*)

PICOS

GRISSINI TORINESI TOPPED WITH
FRESH ROSEMARY, COARSE SEA SALT
AND SESAME SEEDS

BAGELS

These chewy, ring-shaped white rolls were once the everyday bread of Eastern European Jews, but have since become equally associated with New York city and the classic breakfast of bagels and cream cheese. Before baking, the bagels are poached; this gives their characteristically shiny, chewy exteriors and dense, tender interiors.

USING A BREAD MACHINE

Use the dough setting (see pages 66–67). Remove the dough after rising and follow steps 5–9.

INGREDIENTS

2 tsp dried yeast

1½ tbsp granulated sugar

350ml (12fl oz) water

500g (1lb) strong white flour, plus extra for kneading

1½ tsp salt

1 Sprinkle the yeast and sugar into 100ml (3½fl oz) of the water in a bowl. Leave for 5 minutes; stir to dissolve. Mix the flour and salt together in a large bowl. Make a well in the centre of the flour and pour in the yeasted water.

2 Pour the remaining water, holding back about half, into the well. Mix in the flour. Stir in the reserved water, as needed, to form a firm, moist dough.

3 Turn the dough out on to a well-floured work surface. Knead until smooth and elastic, about 10 minutes. As you knead the dough, gradually work in as much additional flour as you can comfortably knead – this dough should be very stiff and firm.

4 Put the dough in a lightly oiled bowl, turning it to coat, and cover with a tea towel. Leave to rise until doubled in size, about 1 hour.

5 Knock back the dough, leave to rest for 10 minutes. Cut into eight pieces. Shape each piece into a ball (*see page 55*). Form each ball into a ring by inserting a floured finger into the centre of each one.

6 Work the finger in a circle to stretch and widen the hole. Then twirl the ring around the index finger of one hand and the thumb of the other hand until the hole is about a third of the bagel's diameter.

7 Place the bagels on a lightly oiled baking sheet, then cover with a damp tea towel and leave to rest for 10 minutes.

8 Bring a large pan of water to the boil, then reduce the heat to allow the water to simmer. Use a perforated skimmer to carefully lower the bagels into the water in batches of two or three at a time. Boil according to the instructions, below.

9 Transfer the drained bagels to a lightly oiled baking sheet. Bake in the preheated oven for 20 minutes or until golden. Leave to cool on a wire rack.

Rising
1 hour
(*see pages 50–51*)

Oven temperature
220°C/425°F/gas 7

Baking
20 minutes
Steam optional
(*see page 63*)

Yield
8 bagels

Yeast alternative
15g (½oz)
fresh yeast
(*see page 41*)

BOILING THE BAGELS

Boil each batch of two or three bagels, uncovered, until they rise to the surface, about 1 minute, turning them once. Remove the bagels from the water using the perforated skimmer, and leave to drain.

SALZBREZELN
PRETZELS

In their native Germany, these twisted, ring-shaped and salt-sprinkled breads are traditionally eaten as a snack with beer, but they make an especially savoury and tasty accompaniment to many drinks. There are two main sorts of pretzel – hard and crisp, and light and chewy. If you prefer your pretzel hard and crisp, omit the final rising after the dough has been shaped.

USING A BREAD MACHINE
Use the dough setting (see pages 66–67). Remove the dough after rising and follow steps 6–8.

INGREDIENTS
2 tsp dried yeast

350ml (12fl oz) water

500g (1lb) strong white flour

1½ tsp salt

egg glaze, made with 1 egg and 1 tbsp water (see page 58)

sesame seeds, poppy seeds, or coarse sea salt, for topping

1 Sprinkle the yeast into 100ml (3½fl oz) of the water in a bowl. Leave for 5 minutes; stir to dissolve. Mix the flour and salt together in a large bowl. Make a well in the centre and pour in the yeasted water.

2 Use a wooden spoon to draw enough of the flour into the yeasted water to form a soft paste. Cover the bowl with a tea towel and leave to "sponge" until frothy and risen, about 20 minutes.

3 Mix in the flour. Stir in the remaining water, as needed, to form a stiff, sticky dough.

4 Turn the dough out on to a lightly floured work surface. Knead until smooth and elastic, about 10 minutes.

5 Put the dough in a bowl and cover with a tea towel. Leave to rise until doubled in size, about 1½–2 hours.

6 Knock back, leave to rest for 10 minutes. Divide into eight pieces. Shape each piece into a round roll and then into an oval (see page 55). Roll each oval backwards and forwards, moving your fingers along the dough, to form a strip about 40cm (16in) long, which is 2.5cm (1in) thick in the middle and 5mm (¼in) thick at each end.

7 Form the shaped dough into pretzels (*see below*). Place the pretzels on a lightly floured baking sheet and cover with a tea towel. Prove until each piece is doubled in size, about 45 minutes.

8 Brush the egg glaze over each pretzel and sprinkle with the topping of your choice. Bake in the preheated oven until golden brown, about 15–20 minutes. Leave to cool on a wire rack.

VARIATION
Salzstangen (Salted Breadsticks)
• Make one quantity Salzbrezeln dough up to step 6.
• Divide the dough into two pieces, then roll each piece into a 30cm (12in) square.
• Using a sharp knife, cut each square in half diagonally, then in half again to form eight triangles. Starting at the widest end, roll up each triangle tightly like a cigar.
• Place the rolled sticks on two lightly floured baking sheets, and cover with a tea towel. Prove until doubled in size, about 40 minutes. Preheat the oven to 220°C/425°F/gas 7.
• Continue as directed in step 8.

To begin
Sponge method
Time: 20 minutes
(*see page 44*)

Rising
1½–2 hours
(*see pages 50–51*)

Proving
45 minutes
(*see page 57*)

Oven temperature
220°C/425°F/gas 7

Baking
15–20 minutes
Steam optional
(*see page 63*)

Yield
8 pretzels

Yeast alternative
15g (½oz)
fresh yeast
(*see page 41*)

FORMING THE PRETZELS

Once the dough has been divided and shaped into strips, pick up the two ends of each strip to make a loop. Cross the ends over twice and then press them down on either side of the dough loop; repeat these actions with each strip of dough.

SOURDOUGHS & OTHER BREADS USING STARTERS

A STARTER ADDS TO THE FLAVOUR and the texture of a loaf. It is made from a small amount of flour, water, and prepared yeast which is left to ferment at room temperature (*see pages 42–43*). The only difference between starter breads and basic breads is in the time required to make them; the methods are the same. Rustic-style sourdough breads are made with starters that require an initial fermentation of at least 48 hours. This produces a bread with a pleasantly sour aroma, hearty texture, and chewy crust. The longer a starter is left to ferment, the more pronounced these qualities are in the baked bread. All starters need to be refrigerated after five days and will keep for up to two weeks. They should be replenished with equal amounts of flour and water after use. In Italy, a starter, or *biga*, traditionally ferments for at least 12 hours. This produces a bread with a lightly fermented flavour, Champagne-like aroma, and open, porous texture. In France, a starter, or *poolish*, traditionally ferments for at least two hours. This shorter fermentation produces a bread with a less yeasty taste, nutty aroma, and springy texture; it has some of the chewiness of a sourdough loaf counter-balanced with the lightness of a basic bread.

PAIN DE CAMPAGNE

PAIN DE CAMPAGNE
FRENCH COUNTRY-STYLE BREAD WITH A SOURDOUGH STARTER

The shaped dough of this classic French loaf is traditionally proved in a basket, which supports it, allowing it to retain its shape before baking. You should place the dough in a basket, about 20cm (8in) in diameter, lined with a well-floured tea towel. Prove as directed in step 7.

USING A BREAD MACHINE

This recipe is not suitable for bread machines.

PROVING IN A BASKET

INGREDIENTS
for the sourdough starter

2 tsp dried yeast
325ml (11fl oz) water
250g (8oz) strong white flour

for the dough

1 tsp dried yeast
200ml (7fl oz) water
50g (1¾oz) rye flour
325g (11oz) strong white flour
1½ tsp salt

1 **To make the starter** Sprinkle the yeast into the water in a large jar. Leave for 5 minutes; stir to dissolve. Stir in the flour using a wooden spoon. Cover the jar with a tea towel and leave to ferment at room temperature for at least 2 days, and at most 3 days. Stir the mixture twice a day; it will be bubbly and pleasantly sour-smelling.

2 **To make the dough** Sprinkle the yeast into the water in a small bowl. Leave for 5 minutes; stir to dissolve. Mix the flours and the salt together in a large bowl and make a well in the centre.

3 Spoon 250ml (8fl oz) of the starter into a liquid measuring jug. Add it to the flour well and pour in the yeasted water. Reserve and replenish the remaining starter (*see right*) in the same jar for the next time you make bread.

4 Mix in the flour from the sides of the well to form a stiff, sticky dough. Add more water 1 tablespoon at a time, if the mixture is too dry.

5 Turn the dough out on to a lightly floured work surface. Knead until smooth and elastic, about 10 minutes.

6 Put the dough in a clean bowl and cover with a tea towel. Leave to rise for 2 hours. Knock back, then leave to rest for 10 minutes.

7 Shape the dough into a round loaf (*see page 54*). Place on a floured baking sheet. Cover with a tea towel and prove until doubled in size, about 1½ hours.

8 Dust the loaf with flour. Cut three parallel slashes (*see page 62*), 5mm (¼in) deep, across the top of the loaf, then three more in the opposite direction. Bake in the preheated oven for 1 hour until golden brown and hollow-sounding when tapped underneath. Leave to cool on a wire rack.

VARIATIONS
Couronne (Crown or Ring Loaf)
(see page 12 for illustration)

• Make one quantity Pain de Campagne dough up to step 7.
• Shape the dough into a couronne shape (*see page 56*).
• Cover the loaf with a tea towel and prove until doubled in size, about 1½ hours. Preheat the oven to 220°C/425°F/gas 7.
• Bake for 45 minutes until hollow-sounding when tapped underneath. Leave to cool on a wire rack.

Pain Tordu
(see page 13 for illustration)

• Make one quantity Pain de Campagne dough up to step 7.
• Shape the dough into a cylinder, 35cm (14in) long. With the handle of a wooden spoon, make an indentation down the centre.
• Twist the dough as if wringing out a cloth. Place on a floured baking sheet and prove for 1½ hours. Preheat the oven to 220°C/425°F/gas 7.
• Bake for 1 hour until hollow-sounding when tapped underneath. Leave to cool on a wire rack.

To begin
Sourdough starter
Time: 2–3 days
(*see page 43*)

Rising
2 hours
(*see pages 50–51*)

Proving
1½ hours
(*see page 57*)

Oven temperature
220°C/425°F/gas 7

Baking
1 hour
Steam optional
(*see page 63*)

Yield
1 loaf

Yeast alternative
For the starter:
15g (½oz)
fresh yeast
For the dough:
5g (¼oz) fresh yeast
(*see page 41*)

MAINTAINING THE STARTER

Place the remaining starter in the glass jar and replenish it with an equal amount of flour and water. If you remove 250ml (8fl oz) of starter to make this recipe, add 125ml (4fl oz) water and 125g (4oz) flour to the jar. This will allow you to keep the sourdough starter fermenting for the next time you make bread. Refer to page 43 for more detailed instructions.

SAN FRANCISCO SOURDOUGH

During the American gold rush, prospectors often carried flour and water in packets strapped to their waists. The mixture would ferment, creating a natural leaven and gave them the nickname "sourbellies". The tradition of sourdough baking has continued and San Franciscans claim their city is the sourdough capital of North America. To maintain a starter, follow the instructions on page 85. (See page 20 for an illustration of the bread.)

USING A BREAD MACHINE

This recipe is not suitable for bread machines.

"OLD" DOUGH

INGREDIENTS

for the starter

3 tsp dried yeast

450ml (¾ pint) water

375g (13oz) strong white flour, sifted

for the dough

175g (6oz) strong white flour

75g (2½ oz) wholemeal flour

2 tsp salt

75g (2½oz) "old" dough
(one piece from recipe below)

1 To make the starter Sprinkle the yeast into the water in a large jar. Leave for 5 minutes; stir to dissolve.

2 Stir the flour into the jar of yeasted water using a wooden spoon. Cover with a tea towel and leave to ferment at room temperature for at least 3 days and at most 5 days before refrigerating. Stir the mixture twice a day; it will be bubbly and pleasantly sour-smelling.

3 To make the dough Mix the flours and salt together in a large bowl. Make a well in the centre. Spoon 500ml (16fl oz) of the starter into a liquid measuring jug. Replenish the remaining starter for the next time you make bread (see page 85). Tear the "old" dough into tiny pieces, then add the starter and the "old" dough pieces to the flour well.

4 Mix in the flour to form a firm but moist dough. Add more water as needed, 1 tablespoon at a time, if the dough is too dry or crumbly.

5 Turn the dough out on to a lightly floured work surface. Knead until smooth and elastic, about 10 minutes.

6 Put the dough in a clean bowl and cover with a tea towel. Leave to rise until doubled in size, about 2 hours. Knock back, then leave to rest for 10 minutes.

7 Pinch off a 75g (2½ oz) piece of the dough for your next breadmaking. Wrap the piece of dough loosely in greaseproof paper and foil and refrigerate or freeze the dough until the next time you make bread (see page 43).

8 Shape the remaining dough into a round loaf (see page 54). Place on a floured baking sheet. Cover with a tea towel and prove until doubled in size, about 1½ hours.

9 Cut three parallel slashes (see page 62), about 5mm (¼in) deep, across the top of the loaf, then three more slashes in the opposite direction to make a criss-cross pattern. Bake in the preheated oven for 1 hour until golden and hollow-sounding when tapped underneath. Leave to cool on a wire rack.

 To begin
Sourdough starter
Time: 3–5 days
(see page 43)

Old dough
Time: 3½ hours
(to make ahead;
see page 43)

 Rising
2 hours
(see pages 50–51)

 Proving
1½ hours
(see page 57)

 Oven temperature
220°C/425°F/gas 7

 Baking
1 hour
Steam optional
(see page 63)

 Yield
1 loaf

 Yeast alternative
For the starter:
25g (1oz)
fresh yeast
(see page 41)

RECIPE FOR "OLD" DOUGH
INGREDIENTS

½ tsp dried yeast or 2.5g (¼oz) fresh yeast

4 tbsp water

100g (3½oz) strong white flour

1 Sprinkle the yeast into the water in a large bowl. Leave for 5 minutes, then stir with a wooden spoon to dissolve.

2 Mix the flour into the yeasted water to form a stiff, sticky dough. Turn the dough out on to a lightly floured work surface. Knead until smooth and elastic, about 10 minutes.

3 Put the dough in a lightly oiled bowl and cover with a tea towel. Leave to rise for 3 hours. Knock back. Divide the dough into two equal pieces. Wrap one piece for future use and add the other piece to the flour well in step 3 of the recipe.

4 "Old" dough can be prepared in advance and frozen (see page 43), or refrigerated. Wrap loosely in greaseproof paper and foil, allowing room for the dough to expand slightly. Defrost, or remove from the refrigerator 1½ hours before use.

PANE DI SEMOLA
SEMOLINA BREAD

This open-textured bread orginates from Puglia, a region of southern Italy, and is commonly known as Pugliese. Its open texture is good for absorbing oil – making it especially popular to use for Bruschetta *(see page 156). Fields of semolina grow profusely in the scorching sun of the region. The semolina flour gives this bread a distinctive golden colour and a crisp crust.*

USING A BREAD MACHINE
This recipe is not suitable for bread machines.

INGREDIENTS
for the starter

¼ tsp dried yeast

175ml (6fl oz) water

125g (4oz) strong white flour

for the dough

1½ tsp dried yeast

175ml (6fl oz) water

125g (4oz) strong white flour

250g (8oz) semolina or durum wheat flour, plus extra to dust

2 tsp salt

2 tbsp olive oil

1 To make the starter Sprinkle the yeast into the water in a bowl. Leave for 5 minutes; stir to dissolve. Add the flour and mix to form a thick batter. Cover with a tea towel and leave to ferment at room temperature for 12–24 hours.

2 To make the dough Sprinkle the yeast into 100ml (3½fl oz) of the water in a small bowl. Leave for 5 minutes; stir to dissolve. Mix the flours and salt together in a large bowl. Make a well in the centre and pour in the yeasted water and the oil, then add the starter.

3 Mix in the flour. Pour in the remaining water as needed to form a soft, sticky dough.

4 Turn the dough out on to a lightly floured work surface. Knead the dough until smooth and elastic, about 10 minutes.

5 Put the dough in a clean, lightly oiled bowl. Leave to rise until doubled in size, 1½–2 hours. Knock back the dough and chafe for 5 minutes (see page 51), then leave to rest for 10 minutes.

6 Divide the dough into two pieces. Shape each piece into a round loaf (see page 54). Place the loaves on an oiled baking sheet dusted with semolina flour.

7 Flatten each loaf with the palm of your hand and sprinkle with semolina flour. Cover with a tea towel and prove until both loaves have doubled in size, about 1½ hours.

8 Bake in the preheated oven for 30 minutes until lightly golden and hollow-sounding when tapped underneath. Leave to cool on a wire rack.

To begin
Starter
Time: 12–24 hours
(see page 42)

Rising
1½–2 hours
(see pages 50–51)

Proving
1½ hours
(see page 57)

Oven temperature
200°C/400°F/gas 6

Baking
30 minutes
Steam optional
(see page 63)

Yield
2 loaves

Yeast alternative
For the starter:
2.5g (⅒oz)
fresh yeast
For the dough:
10g (⅓oz)
fresh yeast
(see page 41)

PANE DI PRATO
TRADITIONAL SALTLESS TUSCAN BREAD

This typical Tuscan bread, also known as Pane Toscano, *is made without salt. During the Middle Ages, Tuscany's neighbouring provinces controlled the Italian salt market, levying a heavy salt tax. Unwilling to submit to their rivals, the Tuscans evolved breads made without salt. The method produces a bread with a yeasty flavour which stales quickly. Tuscan cooks have developed a tradition of dishes using stale bread (see pages 156–157).*

USING A BREAD MACHINE

This recipe is not suitable for bread machines.

INGREDIENTS
for the starter

3½ tsp dried yeast

150ml (¼ pint) water

150g (5oz) strong white flour

for the dough

400g (14oz) strong white flour

300ml (10fl oz) water

1 To make the starter Sprinkle the yeast into the water in a bowl. Leave for 5 minutes; stir to dissolve. Add the flour and mix to form a thick paste. Cover with a tea towel and leave to ferment at room temperature for at least 12 hours.

2 To make the dough Put the flour in a large bowl. Make a well in the centre and add the starter. Pour in the water, holding back about half. Mix in the flour from the sides of the well, then stir in the reserved water to form a wet, batter-like dough.

3 Cover the bowl with a tea towel and leave to rise until doubled in size, about 40 minutes.

4 Turn the dough out on to a well-floured work surface. Use floured hands and a plastic dough scraper to knead the dough until smooth and elastic, about 10 minutes (*see below, right*). Work in additional flour only if necessary to achieve a manageable, but still very moist dough.

5 Divide the dough into two pieces. Handle the dough carefully so as not to deflate it. Shape each piece into an oval loaf (*see page 55*). Place on an oiled baking sheet and cover with a tea towel. Prove until doubled in size, about 15–20 minutes.

6 Sieve a light dusting of flour over the two loaves. Bake in the preheated oven for 35 minutes until lightly golden and hollow-sounding when tapped underneath. Leave to cool on a wire rack.

 To begin
Starter
Time: 12 hours
(*see page 42*)

 Rising
40 minutes
(*see pages 50–51*)

 Proving
15–20 minutes
(*see page 57*)

 Oven temperature
190°C/375°F/gas 5

 Baking
35 minutes
Steam optional
(*see page 63*)

 Yield
2 small loaves

 Yeast alternative
For the starter:
30g (1oz)
fresh yeast
(*see page 41*)

KNEADING A WET DOUGH

A well-floured work surface and hands are necessary when kneading a wet, batter-like dough. Handle the dough with slow, gentle movements. Use a plastic dough scraper to carefully push and turn it. After kneading, the dough should still be soft and pliable.

PANE CASALINGO
ITALIAN "HOUSEHOLD" BREAD

In Italy, "casalingo" describes the very best of family cooking, passed down from mother to daughter. Pane Casalingo *literally means "home-baked" bread and one that is never found in bakeries. It is common all over Italy, from north to south, which is very unusual in the fiercely proud regional cookery of Italy. The starter is uniquely made with malt and milk. This combination speeds up the fermentation of the yeast, giving the loaf a slightly yeasty flavour.*

USING A BREAD MACHINE

This recipe is not suitable for bread machines.

INGREDIENTS
for the starter

1¼ tsp dried yeast

60ml (2fl oz) water

125ml (4fl oz) tepid milk

1 tsp malt extract

200g (7oz) strong white flour

for the dough

1¼ tsp dried yeast

200ml (7fl oz) water

300g (10oz) strong white flour

2 tsp salt

1 To make the starter Sprinkle the yeast into the water and milk in a bowl. Leave for 5 minutes, then add the malt extract and stir to dissolve. Add the flour and mix to form a thick paste. Cover with a tea towel and leave to ferment for 12 hours.

2 To make the dough Sprinkle the yeast into 100ml (3½fl oz) of the water in a bowl. Leave for 5 minutes; stir to dissolve. Mix the flour and the salt together in a large bowl. Make a well in the centre, and add the yeasted water and the starter.

3 Pour half of the remaining water into the well. Mix in the flour. Stir in the reserved water, as needed, to form a soft dough.

4 Turn the dough out on to a well-floured work surface. Knead for 5 minutes. Cover with a tea towel, allow to rest for 10 minutes, then knead for a further 5 minutes.

5 Put the dough in a clean bowl and cover with a tea towel. Leave to rise until trebled in size, about 2 hours. Knock back and chafe for 5 minutes (*see page 51*), then rest for 10 minutes.

6 Shape the dough into a round loaf (*see page 54*). Place on an oiled baking sheet. Cover with a tea towel and leave to prove until doubled in size, about 1½ hours.

7 Dust with flour. Cut three parallel slashes (*see page 62*), ½cm (¼in) deep across the top of the loaf, then three more in the opposite direction to make a criss-cross pattern. Bake in the preheated oven for 50 minutes until hollow-sounding when tapped underneath. Leave to cool on a wire rack.

To begin
Starter
Time: 12 hours
(*see page 42*)

Rising
2 hours
(*see pages 50–51*)

Proving
1½ hours
(*see page 57*)

Oven temperature
200°C/400°F/gas 6

Baking
50 minutes
Steam optional
(*see page 63*)

Yield
1 loaf

Yeast alternative
For the starter:
10g (⅓oz)
fresh yeast
For the dough:
10g (⅓oz)
fresh yeast
(*see page 41*)

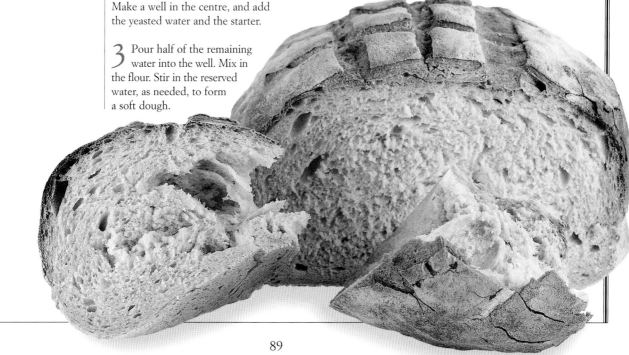

CIABATTA
ITALIAN "SLIPPER" BREAD

Ciabatta *was given its name because the bread resembles a well-worn slipper. Prolonged rising and plenty of liquid produce a very light bread with a uniquely open, porous texture. An authentic* Ciabatta *requires a very wet dough that can be tricky to handle and must be started a day in advance. Do not add extra flour to make the dough more manageable, and avoid overhandling the dough at all costs. After its long rise, the dough must be handled with a very light touch ("like a baby", as they say in Italy), so that none of the precious air bubbles are knocked out.*

USING A BREAD MACHINE
This recipe is not suitable for bread machines.

INGREDIENTS
for the starter
½ tsp dried yeast

150ml (¼ pint) water

3 tbsp tepid milk

¼ tsp honey or granulated sugar

150g (5oz) strong white flour

for the dough
½ tsp dried yeast

250ml (8fl oz) water

½ tbsp olive oil

350g (12oz) strong white flour

1½ tsp salt

1 To make the starter Sprinkle the yeast into the water and milk in a large bowl. Leave for 5 minutes, then add the honey or sugar and stir to dissolve.

2 Mix in the flour to form a loose batter. Cover the bowl with a tea towel and leave to rise for 12 hours or overnight.

3 To make the dough Sprinkle the yeast into the water in a small bowl. Leave for 5 minutes, then stir to dissolve. Add the yeasted water and olive oil to the starter and mix well.

4 Mix in the flour and salt to form a wet, sticky dough. Beat steadily with a wooden spoon for 5 minutes; the dough will become springy and start to pull away from the sides of the bowl, but will remain too soft to knead.

5 Cover the dough with a tea towel. Leave to rise until trebled in size and full of air bubbles, about 3 hours. Do not knock the dough back. Generously flour two baking sheets and have extra flour to dip your hands in.

6 Use a dough scraper to divide the dough in half while in the bowl. Scoop half of the dough out of the bowl on to one of the heavily floured baking sheets.

7 Use well-floured hands to pull and stretch the dough to form a roughly rectangular loaf, about 30cm (12in) long. Dust the loaf and your hands again with flour. Neaten and plump up the loaf by running your fingers down each side and gently tucking the edges of the dough under (*see below*).

8 Repeat step 7 with the other half of the dough. Leave the two loaves uncovered to prove, about 20 minutes; the loaves will spread out as well as rise.

9 Bake in the preheated oven for 30 minutes until risen, golden, and hollow-sounding when tapped underneath. Leave to cool on a wire rack.

To begin
Starter
Time: 12 hours or overnight
(*see page 42*)

Rising
3 hours
(*see pages 50–51*)

Proving
20 minutes
(*see page 57*)

Oven temperature
220°C/425°F/gas 7

Baking
30 minutes
Steam optional
(*see page 63*)

Yield
2 loaves

Yeast alternative
For the starter:
2.5g (⅒oz) fresh yeast
For the dough:
2.5g (⅒oz) fresh yeast
(*see page 41*)

SHAPING CIABATTA

Use well-floured hands to neaten and plump up the loaf by running your fingers down each side and gently tucking the edges of the dough under.

LANDBROT
GERMAN COUNTRY-STYLE RYE BREAD

Rye was traditionally the most important of all grain crops to Germany, and German bakers remain the undisputed masters of rye breads. Landbrot translates literally as "bread of the land", and it is the German equivalent of Pain de Campagne. It is baked throughout Germany, and although there are regional differences in colour and texture, because the proportions of rye to wheat vary, it is usually dusted with flour. (See page 18 for an illustration of the bread.)

USING A BREAD MACHINE
This recipe is not suitable for bread machines.

INGREDIENTS
for the starter
½ tsp dried yeast

3 tbsp water

50g (1¼oz) strong white flour

1 tbsp milk

for the dough
1½ tsp dried yeast

350ml (12fl oz) water

350g (12oz) rye flour

100g (3½oz) strong white flour

2 tsp salt

1 **To make the starter** Sprinkle the yeast into the water in a bowl. Leave for 5 minutes; stir to dissolve. Mix in the flour and milk. Cover with a tea towel and leave to ferment at room temperature for 12–18 hours. The mixture will be bubbly and pleasantly sour-smelling.

2 **To make the dough** Sprinkle the yeast into 250ml (8fl oz) of the water in a bowl. Leave for 5 minutes; stir to dissolve. Mix the flours together in a large bowl. Make a well in the centre and add the yeasted water and starter.

3 Use a wooden spoon to draw enough of the flour into the starter mixture to form a thick batter. Cover the bowl with a tea towel and leave to "sponge" until frothy and risen, 12–18 hours.

4 Add the salt to the fermented batter, then mix in the flour. Stir in the reserved water, as needed, to form a stiff, sticky dough.

5 Turn the dough out on to a lightly floured work surface. Knead until smooth and elastic, about 10 minutes. Leave to rest for a further 10 minutes.

6 Shape the dough into a round loaf (see page 54). Place on a floured baking sheet. Dust the loaf with flour. Cut one slash, 1cm (½in) deep, across the top of the loaf, then another in the opposite direction to make an "X" (see page 62).

7 Cover with a tea towel and prove until doubled in size, about 1½ hours.

8 Bake in the preheated oven for 1¼ hours until hollow-sounding when tapped underneath. Leave to cool on a wire rack.

VARIATIONS
Seeded German Rye Bread
• Combine 2 tablespoons each linseeds, sesame seeds, and pumpkin seeds in a food processor. Using the pulse button process until roughly chopped. Alternatively, grind by hand using a pestle and mortar.
• Make one quantity Landbrot dough up to step 4.
• Add the seed mixture with the salt to the fermented batter. Continue as directed in steps 4–5.
• Shape the dough for a greased 1kg (2lb) loaf tin (see page 53).
• Prove as directed in step 7. Preheat the oven to 200°C/400°F/gas 6.
• Brush with milk and sprinkle with whole linseeds, sesame seeds, and pumpkin seeds.
• Bake as directed in step 8.

Rye Bread with Caraway Seeds
• Make one quantity Landbrot dough adding ½ teaspoon caraway seeds to the starter in step 1.
• Shape the dough for a greased 1kg (2lb) loaf tin (see page 53).
• Prove as directed in step 7. Preheat the oven to 200°C/400°F/gas 6.
• Brush with milk and sprinkle evenly with 2 tablespoons rye flakes over the top of the loaf.
• Bake as directed in step 8.

To begin
Starter
Time: 12–18 hours
(see page 42)

Sponge method
Time: 12–18 hours
(see page 44)

Proving
1½ hours
(see page 57)

Oven temperature
200°C/400°F/gas 6

Baking
1¼ hours
Steam optional
(see page 63)

Yield
1 loaf

Yeast alternative
For the starter:
2.5g (⅙oz) fresh yeast
For the dough:
10g (⅓oz) fresh yeast
(see page 41)

PAIN DE SEIGLE
FRENCH RYE BREAD

In France, rye bread originated in mountainous regions, such as the Alps, Pyrenees, and Vosges, where it was a staple, everyday bread. Today, rye bread is eaten more infrequently, but it is always served, thinly sliced and thickly buttered, as an accompaniment to oysters or the gargantuan plateau de fruits de mer, which is a speciality of the brasseries of Paris.

USING A BREAD MACHINE
This recipe is not suitable for bread machines.

INGREDIENTS
for the starter

2 tsp dried yeast
150ml (¼ pint) water
125g (4oz) strong white flour

for the dough

75g (2½oz) strong white flour
300g (10oz) rye flour
2 tsp salt
250ml (8fl oz) water

1 To make the starter Sprinkle the yeast into the water in a bowl. Leave for 5 minutes; stir to dissolve. Add the flour and mix to form a thick batter. Cover with a tea towel and leave for 2 hours.

2 To make the dough Mix the flours and the salt together in a large bowl. Make a well in the centre and pour in the starter and half of the water.

3 Mix in the flour. Stir in the remaining water to form a fairly moist, sticky dough.

4 Turn the dough out on to a lightly floured work surface. Knead the dough until smooth and elastic, about 10 minutes.

5 Put the dough in a clean bowl and cover with a tea towel. Leave to rise until doubled in size, about 1 hour. Knock back, then leave to rest for 10 minutes.

6 Divide the dough into two pieces and shape each piece into a long loaf (*see pages 52–53*), about 30cm (12in) in length. Place the loaves on a floured baking sheet and leave to rest for 5 minutes.

7 Lightly dust the loaves with flour. Cut six or seven short, parallel slashes, 5mm (¼in) deep, at 1cm (½in) intervals, down both sides of the loaves (*see page 62*). Cover with a tea towel and prove until doubled in size, about 1½ hours.

8 Bake in the preheated oven for 45 minutes until hollow-sounding when tapped underneath. Leave to cool on a wire rack.

To begin
Starter
Time: 2 hours
(*see page 42*)

Rising
1 hour
(*see pages 50–51*)

Proving
1½ hours
(*see page 57*)

Oven temperature
200°C/400°F/gas 6

Baking
45 minutes
Steam optional
(*see page 63*)

Yield
2 small loaves

Yeast alternative
15g (½oz)
fresh yeast
(*see page 41*)

FLAVOURED BREADS

ADDING FLAVOURINGS TO A BASIC DOUGH
ALLOWS THE BAKER TO VARY THE TASTE,
TEXTURE, AND COLOUR OF A BREAD. FLAVOURINGS
ARE EITHER INCORPORATED DURING MIXING
OR ADDED TO A KNEADED DOUGH. LIGHT
INGREDIENTS, SUCH AS HERBS AND SPICES, WHICH
DO NOT INHIBIT THE DOUGH'S RISING, ARE ADDED
WITH THE FLOUR AT THE MIXING STAGE. MOIST
INGREDIENTS, SUCH AS GRATED OR PUREED
VEGETABLES OR COOKED WHOLE GRAINS, WHICH
ALSO SUPPLY SOME OF THE DOUGH'S LIQUID
CONTENT, ARE ALSO ADDED BEFORE RISING.
HEAVIER INGREDIENTS SUCH AS NUTS TEND TO
BE KNEADED IN AFTER THE DOUGH HAS RISEN SO
AS NOT TO HINDER THE ACTION OF THE YEAST.
ALTERNATIVELY, A BASIC DOUGH MAY BE TOPPED
OR FILLED JUST BEFORE BAKING.

LEFT **CARROT BREAD IN
A VARIETY OF FLAVOUR VARIATIONS**

CARROT BREAD

Adding shredded raw vegetables enhances a bread's colour, texture, and flavour. Grated carrot makes a most attractive savoury loaf, and grated raw beetroot contributes dramatic colouring. Both grated raw vegetables and cooked vegetable purées can be worked into this dough with great success.

USING A BREAD MACHINE

This bread may be made entirely in a machine. Follow the manufacturer's instructions (see pages 66–67).

INGREDIENTS

2 tsp dried yeast

350ml (12fl oz) water

500g (1lb) strong white flour

2 tsp salt

250g (8oz) carrots, grated

15g (½oz) unsalted butter, melted

1 Sprinkle the yeast into 100ml (3½fl oz) of the water. Leave for 5 minutes; stir to dissolve.

2 Mix the flour and salt together in a large bowl. Make a well in the centre and pour in the yeasted water. Add the carrots and butter to the well. Mix in the flour. Stir in the remaining water, as needed, to form a moist, crumbly dough.

3 Turn the dough out on to a lightly floured work surface. Knead the dough until smooth but still sticky, about 10 minutes.

4 Put the dough in a clean bowl and cover with a tea towel. Leave to rise until doubled in size, about 1–1½ hours. Knock back, then leave to rest for 10 minutes.

5 Shape the dough into a round loaf (*see page 54*). Place on a floured baking sheet and cover with a tea towel. Prove until doubled in size, about 45 minutes.

6 Bake in the preheated oven for 45 minutes until golden and hollow-sounding when tapped underneath. Cool on a wire rack.

VARIATIONS
Spinach Bread
• Immerse 150g (5oz) spinach in rapid boiling water.
• When the water returns to the boil, drain and rinse the spinach in cold water; squeeze dry.
• In a food processor or blender, purée the spinach, about 1 minute.
• Put the purée in a measuring jug and pour in enough water to make up a volume of 250ml (8fl oz).
• Make one quantity Carrot Bread dough up to step 4, replacing the grated carrot and remaining water with the spinach purée liquid in step 2. Pour the spinach purée liquid into the flour well to form a moist, crumbly dough.
• Continue as directed in steps 4–6.

Beetroot Bread
• Make one quantity Carrot Bread dough up to step 4, replacing the grated carrot with grated raw beetroot in step 2.
• Continue as directed in steps 4–6.

Herb Bread
• Make one quantity Carrot Bread dough up to step 4, replacing the grated carrot with a handful of finely chopped herbs in step 2. Choose parsley for colour, and use in combination with either rosemary and thyme, or chives and marjoram.
• Continue as directed in steps 4–6.

Chilli Bread
• Make one quantity Carrot Bread dough up to step 4, replacing the carrots with 3 teaspoons chilli flakes. Mix these in with the flour and salt in step 2.
• Continue as directed in steps 4–6.

Onion and Caraway Bread
• Melt 60g (2oz) butter in a pan over a medium heat. Add 1 onion, chopped. Cook for 10 minutes until soft and golden.
• Make one quantity Carrot Bread dough up to step 4, using the onion and 1 tablespoon caraway seeds instead of the carrots.
• Continue as directed in steps 4–6.

Rising
1–1½ hours
(*see pages 50–51*)

Proving
45 minutes
(*see page 57*)

Oven temperature
200°C/400°F/gas 6

Baking
45 minutes
Steam optional
(*see page 63*)

Yield
1 loaf

Yeast alternative
15g (½oz)
fresh yeast
(*see page 41*)

PUMPKIN BREAD

This is a slightly sweet, light-textured bread with a soft crust and a rich, golden crumb. When fresh pumpkins are not available, canned pumpkin purée will work just as well. Use water as a substitute for the reserved cooking liquid.

USING A BREAD MACHINE

If you wish to omit the pumpkin seeds and egg glaze, this bread may be made entirely in a machine. Follow the manufacturer's instructions (see pages 66–67).

PUMPKIN BREAD

INGREDIENTS

500g (1lb) pumpkin, peeled, seeded, and cut into pieces, or 300g (10oz) canned pumpkin purée

2 tsp dried yeast

2 tsp runny honey

500g (1lb) strong white flour

2 tsp salt

egg glaze, made with 1 egg yolk and 1 tbsp milk (see page 58)

2 tbsp pumpkin seeds, to decorate

1 Bring a large pan of salted water to the boil. Add the pumpkin flesh and simmer steadily until soft and cooked through, about 20 minutes. Drain the pumpkin well and reserve the cooking liquid.

2 Mash the pumpkin thoroughly, and sieve, or purée in a food processor or blender, about 2 minutes. Leave the pumpkin purée and the reserved cooking liquid to cool until tepid.

3 Sprinkle the yeast into 60ml (2fl oz) of the reserved cooking liquid (or water, if using canned pumpkin purée). Leave for 5 minutes; add the honey and stir to dissolve.

4 Mix the flour and salt in a large bowl. Make a well in the centre. Add the yeasted liquid and honey, then the pumpkin (*see below, right*).

5 Gradually mix in the flour to form a fairly firm, coarse, sticky dough. If the mixture is too dry, add a few tablespoons of the pumpkin cooking liquid (or water if using canned pumpkin).

6 Turn the dough out on to a lightly floured work surface. Knead until very smooth, silky, and elastic, about 10 minutes.

7 Put the dough in a clean bowl and cover with a tea towel. Leave to rise until doubled in size, about 1½ hours. Knock back, then leave to rest for 10 minutes.

8 Shape the dough into a round loaf (*see page 54*). Place on an oiled baking sheet and cover with a tea towel. Prove until doubled in size, about 1 hour.

9 Brush the dough with the egg glaze and sprinkle with pumpkin seeds. Bake in the preheated oven for 40 minutes until golden-coloured and hollow-sounding when tapped underneath. Leave to cool on a wire rack.

 Rising
1½ hours
(*see pages 50–51*)

 Proving
1 hour
(*see page 57*)

 Oven temperature
220°C/425°F/gas 7

 Baking
40 minutes
Steam optional
(*see page 63*)

 Yield
1 loaf

 Yeast alternative
15g (½oz)
fresh yeast
(*see page 41*)

MIXING IN THE FLAVOURING

Add the pumpkin purée directly to the flour well after the yeasted liquid.

PAIN AU FROMAGE

CHEESE HEARTH BREAD

This cheese-enriched, crusty bread from southern France was traditionally baked in a hearth on the dying embers of a fire. It is a perfect casse-croute *(which means snack, or literally "break-crust"). Serve it with a few juicy black olives, a slice of* jambon de pays, *and a glass of red wine.*

USING A BREAD MACHINE
This recipe is not suitable for bread machines.

PAIN AU FROMAGE

INGREDIENTS
2 tsp dried yeast

350ml (12fl oz) water

500g (1lb) strong white flour

1½ tsp salt

1 tbsp olive oil

250g (8oz) Gruyère, grated, plus extra for topping (optional)

1 Sprinkle the yeast into 100ml (3½fl oz) of the water in a bowl. Leave for 5 minutes; stir to dissolve. Mix the flour and salt together in a large bowl. Make a well in the centre of the flour and pour in the yeasted water and olive oil.

2 Use a wooden spoon to draw enough of the flour into the yeasted water to form a thick paste. Cover the bowl with a tea towel, then leave to "sponge" until frothy and risen, about 20 minutes.

3 Pour the remaining water, holding back about half, into the well. Mix in the flour. Stir in the reserved water, as needed, to form a firm, moist dough.

4 Turn the dough out on to a lightly floured work surface. Knead until smooth and elastic, about 10 minutes. Knead in the grated cheese (*see page 99*).

5 Put the dough in a clean bowl and cover with a tea towel. Leave to rise until doubled in size, about 1½ hours. Knock back, then leave to rest for 10 minutes.

6 Divide the dough into four equal pieces by flattening it into a round and cutting it into quarters. Leave to rest for 10 minutes.

7 Roll out each piece of dough into a flat, oval shape, about 5mm (¼in) thick. If the dough resists rolling out, allow it to rest for 1–2 minutes. Transfer the dough on to two greased baking sheets.

8 With a sharp knife make five slashes through each piece of dough, beginning and ending each cut about 2.5cm (1in) from the edge of the dough. Open up each slash by gently pulling the edges apart. Cover with a tea towel and prove the dough, until expanded and slightly puffy, about for 45 minutes.

9 Sprinkle with additional grated cheese, if desired. Bake in the preheated oven for 25–30 minutes until crisp, golden, and hollow-sounding when tapped underneath. Cool on a wire rack.

VARIATION
Pain aux Olives (Olive Hearth Bread)
• Make one quantity Pain au Fromage dough, replacing the Gruyère with 150g (5oz) roughly chopped, pitted green olives in step 4.
• Decorate the shaped dough with more sliced olives instead of the cheese prior to baking in step 9.

To begin
Sponge method
Time: 20 minutes
(*see page 44*)

Rising
1½ hours
(*see pages 50–51*)

Proving
45 minutes
(*see page 57*)

Oven temperature
200°C/400°F/gas 6

Baking
25–30 minutes
Steam optional
(*see page 63*)

Yield
4 loaves

Yeast alternative
15g (½oz)
fresh yeast
(*see page 41*)

PAIN AUX OLIVES

PAIN AUX NOIX
WALNUT BREAD

Walnut bread goes especially well with goat's cheese, as well as the blue-veined sheep's milk cheese, Roquefort. Any leftovers can be toasted to make Croûtes (see page 161) for a warm goat's cheese salad.

USING A BREAD MACHINE

If your machine has a nut dispenser, you may be able to make this entirely in a machine. Refer to your manufacturer's instructions and see pages 66–67.

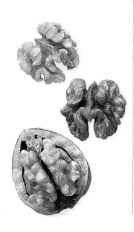

INGREDIENTS

2 tsp dried yeast

350ml (12fl oz) water

250g (8oz) strong white flour

125g (4oz) rye flour

125g (4oz) wholemeal flour

2 tsp salt

150g (5oz) walnut halves, roughly chopped

1 Sprinkle the yeast into 100ml (3½fl oz) of the water in a bowl. Leave for 5 minutes; stir to dissolve. Mix the flours and the salt together in a bowl. Make a well in the centre and pour in the yeasted water.

2 Use a wooden spoon to draw enough of the flour into the yeasted water to form a thick paste. Cover the bowl with a tea towel, then leave to "sponge" until frothy and risen, about 20 minutes.

3 Pour the remaining water, holding back about half, into the well. Mix in the flour. Stir in the reserved water, as needed, to form a firm, moist dough.

4 Turn out on to a floured work surface. Knead until smooth and elastic, about 10 minutes. Add the walnuts at the end of kneading (*see below, left and right*).

5 Put the dough in a clean bowl and cover with a tea towel. Leave to rise until doubled in size, about 1½–2 hours. Knock back, then leave to rest for 10 minutes.

6 Shape the dough into a long loaf, about 25cm (10in) in length (*see page 52*). Place the shaped dough on a floured baking sheet, and cover with a tea towel. Prove until doubled in size, about 45 minutes.

7 Bake in the preheated oven for 45 minutes–1 hour until the loaf is hollow-sounding when tapped underneath. Cool on a wire rack.

VARIATION
Pain aux Pruneaux et Noisette (Prune and Hazelnut Bread)

• Make one quantity Pain aux Noix dough up to step 5, replacing the walnuts with 75g (2½oz) each of whole hazelnuts and quartered dried prunes.
• Leave to rise until doubled in size, about 1½–2 hours. Knock back.
• Shape the dough as directed in step 6, then lightly press three additional whole prunes in a row on top of the loaf to decorate.
• Prove until doubled in size, about 45 minutes. Preheat the oven to 200°C/400°F/gas 6.
• Bake as directed in step 7.

 To begin
Sponge method
Time: 20 minutes
(*see page 44*)

 Rising
1½–2 hours
(*see pages 50–51*)

 Proving
45 minutes
(*see page 57*)

 Oven temperature
200°C/400°F/gas 6

 Baking
45 minutes–1 hour
Steam optional
(*see page 63*)

 Yield
1 loaf

Yeast alternative
15g (½oz)
fresh yeast
(*see page 41*)

KNEADING IN COARSE INGREDIENTS

In step 4, allow the dough to rest for about 5 minutes so that it will be easier to knead. Gently press the dough into a round, about 2.5cm (1in) thick. Sprinkle the walnuts over the surface. Fold the dough in half (see right).

Then gently knead the dough to evenly distribute the ingredients, about 2–4 minutes. The dough will separate and look crumbly before it comes together to form a smooth mass (see left).

MULTIGRAIN BREAD

MULTIGRAIN ROLLS

This healthy, modern American classic has a nutty flavour and a crunchy texture from the addition of seven different ground and whole grains. Various brands of multigrain cereal are available at health food stores but you can mix your own equally well; the seven whole grains used here are oats, brown rice, triticale, rye, wheat, buckwheat, barley, and sesame seeds, but millet, soya, and linseeds are other possibilities.

USING A BREAD MACHINE

This bread may be made entirely in a machine if the topping is omitted. Follow the manufacturer's instructions (see pages 66–67).

INGREDIENTS

2 tsp dried yeast

350ml (12fl oz) water

300g (10oz) strong white flour

200g (7oz) strong wholemeal flour

100g (3½oz) seven-grain cereal, ground

2 tsp salt

2 tbsp linseed or sunflower oil

2 tbsp runny honey

200g (7oz) cooked seven-grain cereal, cooled

oat flakes or rolled oats, for topping

1 Grease a 1kg (2lb) loaf tin with vegetable oil. Sprinkle the yeast into the water in a bowl. Leave for 5 minutes; stir to dissolve.

2 Mix the flours, ground grains, and salt together in a large bowl. Make a well in the centre and pour in the yeast mixture, oil, honey, and cooked grains. Stir in the flour to form a stiff dough.

3 Turn the dough out on to a lightly floured work surface. Knead the dough until glossy and elastic, about 10 minutes.

4 Put the dough in a large, lightly oiled bowl. Turn the dough in the bowl to coat with the oil and cover with a tea towel. Leave to rise until doubled in size, about 1 hour. Knock back the dough, then leave to rest for a further 10 minutes.

5 Shape the dough for a loaf tin (see page 53), and place in the tin, seam-side down. Cover loosely with a tea towel. Prove until doubled in size, about 30 minutes.

6 Brush the top of the loaf with water and sprinkle a generous covering of oat flakes or rolled oats over the top to finish the loaf.

7 Bake in the preheated oven for 40 minutes. Turn the loaf out of the tin, and return it to the oven bottom-side up for 5 minutes more. Leave to cool on a wire rack.

VARIATIONS

Sunflower and Honey Bread

• Make one quantity Multigrain Bread dough, replacing the ground and cooked seven-grain cereal with 125g (4oz) sunflower seeds and 2 tablespoons wheatgerm. Add to the well as directed in step 2 and increase the amount of honey from 2 to 3 tablespoons.
• Continue up to step 6.
• Sprinkle the loaf with sunflower seeds, instead of the oat flakes.
• Bake as directed in step 7.

Cracked Grain Bread

• Put 75g (2½ oz) each cracked buckwheat, cracked wheat, and cracked rye in a bowl; pour over boiling water to cover. Leave for 30 minutes until swollen, then drain.
• Make one quantity Multigrain Bread dough, replacing the seven-grain cereal with the cracked grains and 2 tablespoons linseeds.
• Continue up to step 6.
• Sprinkle the top of the loaf with 2 tablespoons sesame seeds, instead of the oat flakes or rolled oats.
• Bake as directed in step 7.

Multigrain Rolls

• Make one quantity Multigrain Bread dough up to step 5.
• Divide the dough into eight pieces and shape into round rolls (see page 55).
• Place on a greased baking sheet; cover with a tea towel. Prove until doubled in size, about 40 minutes.
• Preheat the oven to 200°C/400°F/gas 6. Use scissors to snip an "X" in each roll (see page 62). Top as directed in step 6, then bake for 30 minutes.

 Rising
1 hour
(see pages 50–51)

 Proving
30 minutes
(see page 57)

 Oven temperature
200°C/400°F/gas 6

 Baking
45 minutes
Steam optional
(see page 63)

 Yield
1 loaf

 Yeast alternative
15g (½oz)
fresh yeast
(see page 41)

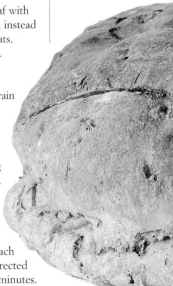

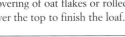

PANE CON POMODORI E CIPOLLE ROSSE

TOMATO AND RED ONION BREAD

This robustly flavoured loaf originated in Tropea in the southern Italian region of Calabria. Ripe, full-flavoured tomatoes are essential to its success. Choose firm, red tomatoes or leave unripe tomatoes stem-side down on a window sill to ripen. Store ripe tomatoes in a dark, cool place, but never refrigerate them.

USING A BREAD MACHINE

This bread may be made entirely in a machine. Follow the manufacturer's instructions (see pages 66–67).

PANE CON POMODORI E CIPOLLE ROSSE

INGREDIENTS

3½ tsp dried yeast

150ml (¼ pint) water

500g (1lb) strong white flour

2 tsp salt

500g (1lb) ripe tomatoes

1 tbsp olive oil

2 red onions, halved and finely sliced

3 tsp chopped fresh oregano

1 tsp dried chilli flakes

1 Sprinkle the yeast into the water in a bowl. Leave for 5 minutes; stir to dissolve. Mix the flour and salt together in a large bowl. Make a well in the centre of the flour and pour in the yeasted water.

2 Use a wooden spoon to draw enough of the flour into the yeasted water to form a thick paste. Cover the bowl with a tea towel and leave to "sponge" until frothy and risen, about 1 hour.

3 To skin the tomatoes, immerse them in boiling water for 1 minute. Score the skin with a knife and peel it away. Cut the tomatoes in half, remove the cores, scoop out the seeds, and roughly chop the flesh. Reserve the flesh only.

4 Heat the olive oil in a pan, then add the tomatoes, sliced onions, oregano, and chilli. Cover the pan and cook gently for 10 minutes. Transfer the tomato mixture to a bowl, and leave to cool.

5 Stir the cooled tomato mixture into the fermented sponge. Mix in the flour to make a soft, sticky dough. The moisture content of the tomatoes will affect the consistency. Add flour if the dough is too wet.

6 Turn the dough out on to a lightly floured work surface. Knead until silky and supple, about 10 minutes.

7 Put the dough in a lightly oiled bowl and cover with a tea towel. Leave to rise until doubled in size, about 1 hour. Knock back, then chafe for 5 minutes; leave to rest for a further 10 minutes.

8 Shape the dough into a round loaf (see page 54). Place on an oiled baking sheet and cover with a tea towel. Leave to prove until doubled in size, about 35–45 minutes.

9 Bake in the preheated oven for 45 minutes until golden and hollow-sounding when tapped underneath. Cool on a wire rack.

To begin
Sponge method
Time: 1 hour
(*see page 44*)

Rising
1 hour
(*see pages 50–51*)

Proving
35–45 minutes
(*see page 57*)

Oven temperature
200°C/400°F/gas 6

Baking
45 minutes
Steam optional
(*see page 63*)

Yield
1 loaf

Yeast alternative
30g (1oz)
fresh yeast
(*see page 41*)

DARK CHOCOLATE BREAD

This savoury, bitter-sweet bread goes well with beef or game stew.

USING A BREAD MACHINE

This bread may be made entirely in a machine (see pages 66–67).

INGREDIENTS

2 tsp dried yeast

400ml (14fl oz) water

4 tbsp caster sugar

400g (14oz) strong white flour

100g (4oz) cocoa powder

1½ tsp salt

1 Sprinkle the yeast into 100ml (3½fl oz) of the water in a bowl. Leave for 5 minutes, then add the sugar; stir to dissolve. Sift the flour, cocoa, and salt together into a large bowl. Make a well in the centre and pour in the yeasted mixture.

2 Pour the remaining water, holding back about half, into the well. Mix in the flour from the sides of the well. Stir in the reserved water, as needed, to form a stiff dough.

3 Turn the dough out on to a lightly floured work surface. Knead until smooth, silky, and elastic, about 10 minutes.

4 Put the dough in a clean bowl and cover with a tea towel. Leave to rise until doubled in size, about 1 hour. Knock back, then leave to rest for 10 minutes.

5 Shape the dough into a round loaf (*see page 54*). Place on a lightly floured baking sheet and cover with a tea towel. Prove until doubled in size, about 45 minutes.

6 Dust the loaf with cocoa powder. Make a series of slashes, 1cm (½in) deep, across the top of the loaf (*see page 62*) to form a decorative pattern. Bake in the preheated oven for 45 minutes until hollow-sounding when tapped underneath. Leave to cool on a wire rack.

 Rising
1 hour
(*see pages 50–51*)

 Proving
45 minutes
(*see page 57*)

 Oven temperature
220°C/425°F/gas 7

 Baking
45 minutes
Steam optional
(*see page 63*)

 Yield
1 loaf

 Yeast alternative
15g (½oz)
fresh yeast
(*see page 41*)

SOUTH AFRICAN SEED BREAD

This seed-packed, super-healthy bread with a nutty, cakey crumb and a soft, golden crust is unique to South Africa. It is a relatively quick yeast bread to make as it requires no kneading and only one rise after the dough has been shaped.

USING A BREAD MACHINE

This recipe is not suitable for bread machines.

INGREDIENTS

unsalted butter, melted, to grease the tin

3 tsp dried yeast

375ml (13fl oz) water

4 tsp runny honey

375g (13oz) wholemeal flour

125g (4oz) strong white flour

3 tbsp each sesame seeds, sunflower seeds, linseeds, poppy seeds, chopped mixed nuts

1½ tsp salt

1 tbsp milk

1 Grease a 500g (1lb) loaf tin with melted butter. Sprinkle the yeast into 300ml (½ pint) of the water in a bowl, and stir in the runny honey. Leave for 5 minutes; stir to dissolve. Mix the flours, seeds, nuts, and salt together in a large bowl.

2 Make a well in the centre of the flour mixture and pour in the yeasted liquid. Mix in the flour from the sides of the well. Stir in the remaining water as needed to form a soft, sticky dough that just begins to leave the sides of the bowl clean.

3 Spoon the dough into the greased tin, then use the back of the spoon to smooth it level. Leave to prove until the dough has risen just above the rim of the tin, 1 hour.

4 Bake in the preheated oven for 30 minutes, then reduce the temperature to 180°C/350°F/gas 4 and bake for a further 30 minutes. The top of the bread will remain flat. Turn out on to a wire rack to cool. Immediately brush the top and sides of the loaf with milk.

 Proving
1 hour
(*see page 57*)

 Oven temperature
200°C/400°F/gas 6

 Baking
1 hour

 Yield
1 loaf

 Yeast alternative
25g (1oz)
fresh yeast
(*see page 41*)

HUNGARIAN POTATO BREAD

Adapted from George Lang's book Cuisine of Hungary, this is an unusual bread, truly worth making. We love its moist, springy crumb and earthy, subtly spiced flavour. During proving the loaf will not rise as much as most doughs due to the denseness of the potatoes. However, once the bread is placed in a hot oven the moisture in the potatoes will cause the loaf to expand dramatically.

USING A BREAD MACHINE

Unless you wish to hand-shape this bread, it may be made entirely in a machine. Follow the manufacturer's instructions (see pages 66–67).

INGREDIENTS

2 medium-sized floury potatoes, peeled (about 500g/1lb)

2 tsp dried yeast

375g (13oz) strong white flour

1½ tsp salt

½ tsp caraway seeds

1 Boil the potatoes until soft, then drain, reserving 175ml (6fl oz) of the cooking water. Mash the potatoes thoroughly, pushing them through a sieve or food mill to form 375g (13oz) of smooth, dry, and fluffy mashed potatoes. Leave the potatoes and the cooking water to cool until tepid.

2 Sprinkle the yeast into 100ml (3½fl oz) of the cooled cooking water in a bowl. Leave for 5 minutes; stir to dissolve. Put the flour in a large bowl. Make a well in the centre and pour in the yeasted liquid.

3 Use a wooden spoon to draw enough of the flour into the yeasted water to form a soft paste. Cover the bowl with a tea towel and leave to "sponge" until frothy and slightly risen, about 20 minutes.

4 Add the mashed potatoes, salt, and caraway seeds to the well.

Mix in the flour thoroughly with a wooden spoon, adding the reserved potato water, as needed, to form a soft, moist dough.

5 Turn the dough out on to a lightly floured work surface. Knead until smooth, shiny, and soft, about 10 minutes.

6 Put the dough in a clean bowl and cover with a tea towel. Leave to rise until doubled in size, about 2 hours. Knock back, then leave to rest for 10 minutes.

7 Shape the dough into a smooth, round loaf (see page 54). Place on a lightly floured baking sheet and cover with a tea towel. Prove until well-risen and the dough springs back slowly when gently pressed with a finger, about 30 minutes.

8 Dust the loaf with flour. Cut three parallel slashes, 1cm (½in) deep, across the top, then three slashes in the opposite direction to make a criss-cross pattern (see page 62).

9 Bake in the preheated oven for 1 hour until crusty and hollow-sounding when tapped underneath. Leave to cool on a wire rack.

 To begin
Sponge method
Time: 20 minutes
(see page 44)

 Rising
2 hours
(see pages 50–51)

 Proving
30 minutes
(see page 57)

 Oven temperature
220°C/425°F/gas 7

 Baking
1 hour
Steam optional
(see page 63)

 Yield
1 loaf

 Yeast alternative
15g (½oz)
fresh yeast
(see page 41)

FOCACCIA FARCITA
FILLED ITALIAN HEARTH BREAD

This Italian bread took its name from the Latin word focus, which means "hearth". The embers of the hearth were where Focaccia was traditionally baked. Fillings and toppings for Focaccia are very much a moveable feast. Generally speaking, Italian-style ingredients such as roasted peppers, sun-dried tomatoes, olives, capers, fragrant fresh herbs, or grilled aubergines, will complement this bread dough to perfection. Bear in mind that any topping or filling must be cooked in the same time that it takes the bread to bake. Therefore, vegetables need to be chopped or sliced, and partially cooked by roasting or parboiling before they can be used.

USING A BREAD MACHINE
Use the dough setting (see pages 66–67). Remove the dough after rising and follow steps 5–9.

INGREDIENTS
2 tsp dried yeast

350ml (12fl oz) water

500g (1lb) strong white flour

1½ tsp salt

3 tbsp olive oil

for the filling and topping
200g (7oz) Gorgonzola, crumbled

200g (7oz) mozzarella, sliced

a handful of basil leaves

½ tsp coarse salt

3 sprigs rosemary, stems removed

4 tbsp olive oil

1 Sprinkle the yeast into 250ml (8fl oz) of the water in a bowl. Leave for 5 minutes; stir to dissolve. Mix the flour and salt together in a large bowl. Make a well in the centre of the flour and pour in the yeasted water and the oil.

2 Mix in the flour. Stir in the remaining water to form a soft, sticky dough. Add more water 1 tablespoon at a time, if needed.

3 Turn the dough out on to a lightly floured work surface. Knead until smooth, silky, and elastic, about 10 minutes.

4 Put the dough in an oiled bowl and cover. Leave to rise until doubled in size, 1½–2 hours.

5 Knock back and divide the dough into two equal pieces. Chafe for 5 minutes (see page 51), then leave to rest for 10 minutes.

6 **The filling** Roll out each piece into a 24cm (9½in) round. Place one on an oiled baking sheet. Arrange the two cheeses and basil over the top, then seal in the filling using the second round (see right).

7 Cover the dough loosely with a tea towel. Prove until doubled in size, about 30 minutes.

8 Use your fingertips to gently press into the surface of the dough to form dimples about 1cm (½in) deep. Sprinkle with the coarse salt and 1 tablespoon of the olive oil, then top with rosemary leaves.

9 Bake in the preheated oven for 30–45 minutes until golden. Drizzle immediately with the remaining olive oil, and serve warm.

VARIATION
Focaccia with Tomato, Rocket and Mozzarella
• Preheat the oven to 200°C/400°F/gas 6. Place 500g (1lb) cherry tomatoes on a baking sheet and sprinkle with 1 tablespoon olive oil. Season with salt and pepper, then bake for 20 minutes.
• Cut 150g (5oz) mozzarella into cherry tomato-sized pieces. Wash and dry 125g (4oz) rocket leaves.
• Make one quantity of Focaccia Farcita dough up to step 6. Replace the filling in step 6 with the tomatoes, mozzarella, and rocket.
• Continue as directed in steps 7–9.

 Rising
1½–2 hours
(see pages 50–51)

 Proving
30 minutes
(see page 57)

 Oven temperature
200°C/400°F/gas 6

 Baking
30–45 minutes
Steam optional
(see page 63)

 Yield
1 loaf

  Yeast alternative
15g (½oz)
fresh yeast
(see page 41)

SEALING IN THE FILLING

To seal the filling, place the second round of dough over the top of the filling. Seal the edges of the dough by gently pinching them together with your fingers.

STROMBOLI

ROLLED HEARTH BREAD FILLED WITH SMOKED MOZZARELLA AND BASIL

This *Focaccia is named after the volcanic island of Stromboli located off the Sicilian coast of Italy. The delicious combination of smoked and plain mozzarella erupts from the pierced holes during baking. Serve still warm from the oven for the most enjoyment.*

USING A BREAD MACHINE

Use the dough setting (see pages 66–67). Remove the dough after rising and follow steps 5–8.

INGREDIENTS

2 tsp dried yeast

350ml (12fl oz) water

500g (1lb) strong white flour

1½ tsp salt

3 tbsp olive oil

for the filling and topping

200g (7oz) mozzarella, chopped

200g (7oz) smoked mozzarella, chopped

1 garlic clove, peeled and chopped

a handful of fresh basil leaves

3 tbsp olive oil

1 tsp coarse sea salt

3 sprigs rosemary, stems removed

1 tsp pepper

1 Sprinkle the yeast into 250ml (8fl oz) of the water in a bowl. Leave for 5 minutes; stir to dissolve.

2 Mix the flour and salt together in a large bowl. Make a well in the centre and pour in the yeasted water and the oil. Mix in the flour from the sides of the well. Stir in the reserved water, as needed, to form a soft, sticky dough.

3 Turn the dough out on to a lightly floured work surface. Knead until smooth, silky, and elastic, about 10 minutes.

4 Put the dough in a clean, oiled bowl and cover with a tea towel. Leave to rise until doubled in size, 1½–2 hours.

5 Knock back, and chafe for 5 minutes (see page 51), then leave to rest for 10 minutes. Shape the dough into a 35cm x 20cm (14in x 8in) rectangle. Cover with a tea towel and leave to rest for 10 minutes.

6 **To make the filling and topping** Spread the cheeses, garlic, and basil leaves evenly over the dough. Roll the dough like a Swiss roll, starting at one of the shorter sides, but without rolling too tightly.

7 Place on an oiled baking sheet. Use a skewer or a carving fork to pierce several holes through the dough to the baking sheet. Sprinkle with 1 tablespoon of the olive oil, salt, rosemary leaves, and pepper.

8 Bake in the preheated oven for 1 hour until golden. Leave to cool slightly, then drizzle over the remaining olive oil.

 Rising
1½–2 hours
(*see pages 50–51*)

 Oven temperature
200°C/400°F/gas 6

 Baking
1 hour
Steam optional
(*see page 63*)

 Yield
1 loaf

 Yeast alternative
15g (½oz)
fresh yeast
(*see page 41*)

FOCACCIA CON OLIVE
HEARTH BREAD WITH OLIVES

Focaccia *originated in Genoa but numerous variations on the classic salt and olive oil Genoese hearth breads are also found all over Liguria. This recipe calls for the famous olives, olive oil, and white wine of the region – the wine in particular adds an extra flavour dimension. This bread is best eaten while still warm.*

INGREDIENTS

2 tsp dried yeast

175ml (6fl oz) water

500g (1lb) strong white flour

1½ tsp salt

75ml (2½fl oz) olive oil, plus additional olive oil to finish

75ml (2½fl oz) dry white wine

200g (7oz) pitted black olives, coarsely chopped

2 tbsp fresh thyme leaves

1 tbsp chopped fresh oregano

1 Sprinkle the yeast into 100ml (3½fl oz) of the water in a bowl. Leave for 5 minutes; stir to dissolve. Mix the flour and salt together in a large bowl. Make a well in the centre and pour in the yeasted water.

2 Use a wooden spoon to draw enough of the flour into the yeasted water to form a soft paste. Cover the bowl with a tea towel, then leave to "sponge" until frothy and risen, about 20 minutes.

3 Add the olive oil and the white wine to the well. Mix in the flour. Stir in the remaining water, as needed, to form a soft, sticky dough.

4 Turn the dough on to a lightly floured surface. Knead until smooth and elastic, about 10 minutes. Work 125g (4oz) of the olives and 1 tablespoon of the thyme leaves into the dough towards the end of kneading (see page 99).

5 Put the dough in an oiled bowl and cover with a tea towel. Leave to rise until doubled in size, 1½–2 hours.

6 Knock back and chafe for 5 minutes (see page 51), then leave to rest for 10 minutes.

7 Roll out the dough on a lightly floured work surface to form a 24cm (9½in) round, 1cm (½in) thick. Place on an oiled baking sheet and cover with a tea towel. Prove until doubled in size, about 1 hour.

8 Use your fingertips to gently press into the surface of the dough to form dimples about 1cm (½in) deep. Sprinkle with the oregano and the remaining olives and thyme.

9 Bake in the preheated oven for 30 minutes until golden brown and hollow-sounding when tapped underneath. Sprinkle with additional oil immediately. Cool on a wire rack.

VARIATION
***Focaccia alla Salvia
(Italian Hearth Bread with Sage)***
• Make one quantity Focaccia con Olive dough up to step 3.
• Add 20 chopped fresh sage leaves to the sponge with the wine and the oil in step 3. Mix in the flour and stir in the water as directed.
• Continue as directed in steps 4–7, replacing the oregano, olives, and thyme with 1½ teaspoons coarse salt, 2 tablespoons olive oil, and 10 fresh sage leaves. Preheat the oven to 200°C/400°F/gas 6.
• Bake as directed in step 9.

To begin
Sponge method
Time: 20 minutes
(see page 44)

Rising
1½–2 hours
(see pages 50–51)

Proving
1 hour
(see page 57)

Oven temperature
200°C/400°F/gas 6

Baking
30 minutes
Steam optional
(see page 63)

Yield
1 loaf

Yeast alternative
15g (½oz)
fresh yeast
(see page 41)

FOCACCIA
ALLA SALVIA

USING A BREAD MACHINE
Use the dough setting (see pages 66–67). Remove after rising and follow steps 6–9. Either add the olives and thyme at the beginning, or remove the dough from the machine after kneading and work them in by hand.

SCHIACCIATA CON LE CIPOLLE ROSSE E FORMAGGIO

SCHIACCIATA WITH ROASTED RED ONIONS AND CHEESE

Schiacciata, *which translates as "squashed", is a Florentine recipe. Light, airy Focaccia is topped with red onions and sharp Gruyère cheese.*

USING A BREAD MACHINE
This recipe is not suitable for bread machines.

INGREDIENTS
for the starter
½ tsp dried yeast

150ml (¼ pint) water

125g (4oz) strong white flour

for the dough
1½ tsp dried yeast

200ml (7fl oz) water

375g (13oz) strong white flour

1½ tsp salt

3 tbsp olive oil

for the topping
3 red onions, each cut into 8 wedges

200g (7oz) Gruyère, grated

2 tsp fresh thyme

4 tbsp olive oil

1 tsp coarse salt

1 **To make the starter** Sprinkle the yeast into the water. Leave for 5 minutes; stir to dissolve. Add the flour and mix to form a thick batter. Cover with a tea towel and leave to ferment at room temperature for at least 12 and up to 36 hours, until it forms a loose, bubbling batter.

2 **To make the dough** Sprinkle the yeast into 100ml (3½fl oz) of the water. Leave for 5 minutes; stir to dissolve. Mix the flour and the salt together in a large bowl. Make a well in the centre of the flour. Pour in the yeasted water, the olive oil, and the starter.

3 Mix in the flour. Stir in the remaining water to form a soft, sticky dough. Add extra water one tablespoon at a time, if necessary.

4 Turn out on to a lightly floured work surface. Knead the dough until smooth, silky and elastic, about 10 minutes.

5 Put the dough in a clean, lightly oiled bowl and cover with a tea towel. Leave to rise until doubled in size, 1½–2 hours. Knock back and chafe for 5 minutes (*see page 51*), then leave to rest, about 10 minutes.

6 Roll out the dough on a lightly floured work surface to form a round, 24cm (9½in) in diameter.

7 Place the dough on a lightly oiled baking sheet and cover with a tea towel. Prove until doubled in size, about 30 minutes.

8 **To make the topping** Use your fingertips to gently press into the dough to make dimples about 1cm (½in) deep. Scatter an even layer of onion wedges and Gruyère on top of the dough, then sprinkle with thyme, oil, and salt.

9 Bake in the preheated oven for 30 minutes until puffed and the topping is crisp. Leave to cool slightly on a wire rack. Cut into wedges and serve while still warm. It is also good at room temperature.

 To begin
Starter
Time: 12–36 hours
(*see page 42*)

 Rising
1½–2 hours
(*see pages 50–51*)

 Proving
30 minutes
(*see page 57*)

 Oven temperature
200°C/400°F/gas 6

 Baking
30 minutes
Steam optional
(*see page 63*)

 Yield
1 loaf

 Yeast alternative
For the starter:
2.5g (¼oz)
fresh yeast
For the dough:
12.5g (½oz)
fresh yeast
(*see page 41*)

SCHIACCIATA CON L'UVA

SCHIACCIATA WITH BLACK GRAPES AND WINE-SOAKED RAISINS

This Schiacciata is traditionally made in Tuscany at grape harvest time with the Sangiovese grapes that are used to make Chianti Classico wines. The raisins inside the dough represent the last season's grapes, while the new season's grapes are used to adorn the top.

USING A BREAD MACHINE
This recipe is not suitable for bread machines.

INGREDIENTS
for the starter

1 quantity starter (see Schiacciata con le Cipolle Rosse e Formaggio, opposite)

for the dough

3 tbsp caster sugar

1 quantity dough (see Schiacciata con le Cipolle Rosse e Formaggio, opposite)

for the filling and topping

200g (7oz) raisins

a glass of Vin Santo or another sweet dessert wine

500g (1lb) seedless black grapes

3 tbsp demerara sugar

1 To make the starter and dough Make the starter and dough as directed for Schiacciata Con le Cipolle Rosse e Formaggio (*see opposite*), up to step 5. Add the caster sugar to the flour and salt in step 2.

2 Put the dough in a lightly oiled bowl and cover with a tea towel. Leave to rise until doubled in size, 1½–2 hours. Knock back and chafe for 5 minutes (*see page 51*), then leave to rest, about 10 minutes.

3 Divide into two equal-sized pieces. Roll out both pieces of dough on a lightly floured work surface to form two rounds, each 24cm (9½in) in diameter. Place one round on a lightly oiled baking sheet.

4 Marinate the raisins in the wine for at least 2 hours or preferably overnight. Drain them thoroughly and reserve the left-over wine as a special treat for the baker.

5 To make the filling Spread the raisins evenly over one round of dough. Put the second round on top and pinch the edges together. Cover with a tea towel, then prove until doubled in size, about 30 minutes.

6 Cover the dough evenly with the grapes, lightly pressing them into the dough, and sprinkle demerara sugar over the top.

7 Bake in the preheated oven for 45 minutes until the crust is golden and the grapes are lightly browned. Cool slightly on a wire rack.

To begin
Starter
Time: 12–36 hours
(*see page 42*)

Rising
1½–2 hours
(*see pages 50–51*)

Proving
30 minutes
(*see page 57*)

Oven temperature
200°C/400°F/gas 6

Baking
45 minutes
Steam optional
(*see page 63*)

Yield
1 loaf

Yeast alternative
For the starter:
2.5g (¼oz)
fresh yeast
For the dough:
12.5g (½oz)
fresh yeast
(*see page 41*)

ENRICHED BREADS

THE ADDITION OF ONE OR MORE ENRICHING INGREDIENTS – SUCH AS BUTTER, OIL, OR EGGS – RESULTS IN A BREAD WITH A SOFT, TENDER CRUMB THAT BECOMES MORE CAKE-LIKE IN DIRECT PROPORTION TO THE QUANTITIES OF THE ENRICHMENTS ADDED. THE MOISTURE IN THESE INGREDIENTS MAKES THE DOUGH SOFT AND OFTEN DIFFICULT TO HANDLE. THE FAT IN THEM COATS THE GLUTEN STRANDS IN THE DOUGH AND CREATES A BARRIER BETWEEN THE FLOUR AND THE YEAST. THIS LENGTHENS THE RISING TIMES SO MUCH THAT IN BREADS LIKE BRIOCHE, THE ENRICHMENTS ARE ADDED AFTER AN INITIAL RISING. THE RECIPES IN THIS SECTION MAY REQUIRE SOME NEW SKILLS AND A BIT MORE CONFIDENCE AND TIME THAN PREVIOUS RECIPES, BUT THEY ARE WORTH IT.

LEFT **AN INDIVIDUAL BRIOCHE AND THE LARGER BRIOCHE A TETE**

BRIOCHE

Egg-and-butter enriched Brioche *dough* is formed into a variety of shapes, but perhaps the classic and most characteristic is that of the small Brioche Parisienne, with its distinctive topknot and scalloped underside. Perhaps best enjoyed at breakfast with raspberry conserve and a steaming bowl of café au lait, the culinary status of Brioche far outstrips the breakfast table. Brioche *dough* is favoured above other doughs and pastries in some celebrated classic dishes, most notably Beef Wellington.

USING A BREAD MACHINE
This bread may be made in a machine which has a double-rising setting (check the manufacturer's instructions). Either make it entirely in the machine or remove the dough after the second kneading and follow steps 7–10.

INGREDIENTS

2½ tsp dried yeast

2 tbsp water

375g (13oz) strong white flour

2 tbsp granulated sugar

1½ tsp salt

5 eggs, beaten

15g (½oz) unsalted butter, melted

175g (6oz) unsalted butter, softened, plus extra to brush moulds

egg glaze, made with 1 egg yolk and 1 tbsp water (see page 58)

1 Sprinkle the yeast into the water in a bowl. Leave for 5 minutes; stir to dissolve. Mix the flour, sugar, and salt together in a large bowl.

2 Make a well in the centre and add the yeasted water and beaten eggs (*see below, left*). Mix in the flour to form a soft, moist but manageable dough.

3 Turn the dough out on to a lightly floured work surface. Knead until elastic, about 10 minutes.

4 Grease a large bowl with the melted butter. Place the dough in the bowl; turn it to coat evenly. Cover with a tea towel and leave to rise until doubled in size, about 1–1½ hours. Knock back, then leave to rest for 10 minutes.

5 Use your hand to incorporate the softened butter into the dough (*see below, right*).

6 Turn out on to a lightly floured work surface. Knead until the butter is distributed throughout, 5 minutes, then rest for 5 minutes more. Grease ten brioche moulds, each about 8cm (3½in) in diameter and 5cm (2in) deep, with the extra softened butter (*see opposite, left*).

7 Divide the dough into ten pieces. Pinch off about a quarter of each piece. Use cupped hands to roll both the large and small pieces of dough into smooth, round balls (*see page 55*). Place one of the large balls in each of the prepared brioche moulds.

8 Use your forefinger to make an indentation in the centre of the large ball, then add the small ball (*see opposite, right*). Repeat this step with the remaining balls of dough.

9 Cover the moulds with a tea towel and prove until the dough has doubled in size, 30 minutes.

10 Brush the tops with the egg glaze. Place the moulds on a baking tray and bake in the preheated oven for 15–20 minutes until glossy and golden. Turn out and leave to cool on a wire rack.

 Rising
1–1½ hours
(*see pages 50–51*)

 Proving
30 minutes
(*see page 57*)

 Oven temperature
220°C/425°F/gas 7

 Baking
15–20 minutes

 Yield
10 small Brioche

 Yeast alternative
20g (¾oz) fresh yeast
(*see page 41*)

ADDING ENRICHMENTS TO DOUGH

In step 2, add beaten eggs directly to the flour well along with the yeasted water. Mix in the flour to form a soft, moist but manageable dough.

In step 5, use your hand to squeeze the softened butter into the dough until evenly distributed throughout.

PREPARING THE MOULD AND DOUGH FOR BAKING

In step 6, grease each mould with softened butter, then place it in the refrigerator. Once the butter has formed a hardened shell, grease each mould a second time with more softened butter.

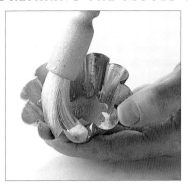

In step 8, use your forefinger to make a slight indentation in the centre of each large ball. Brush the indentation with egg glaze. Place a smaller ball on top to make a topknot.

VARIATIONS
Brioche à Tête
(Large Brioche with a Topknot)
• Make one quantity Brioche dough up to step 7, replacing the ten small moulds in step 6 with a buttered brioche mould, about 18cm (7in) in diameter and 15cm (6in) deep.
• Pinch off a third of the dough. Shape the large piece of dough into a round loaf (*see page 54*). Use cupped hands to roll the small piece into a round roll (*see page 55*).
• Put the large ball, seam-side down, into the brioche mould. Make an indentation, then add the small ball.
• Cover with a tea towel and prove, about 45 minutes. Preheat the oven to 220°C/425°F/gas 7.
• Brush the dough with the egg glaze. Bake for 35–45 minutes until glossy and golden. Turn out of the brioche mould on to a wire rack to cool.

Brioche Nanterre
(Brioche from Nanterre)
• Make one quantity Brioche dough up to step 7, replacing the ten small moulds in step 6 with a buttered 1kg (2lb) loaf tin.
• Divide the dough into eight pieces. Use cupped hands to roll each piece into a round ball (*see page 55*).
• Put the eight rolls of dough in the prepared loaf tin, placing them four in a row down each side of the tin.
• Cover the moulds with a tea towel and prove until the dough fills the tin, about 45 minutes. Preheat the oven to 200°C/400°F/gas 6.

• Brush with the egg glaze. Bake for 35 minutes until shiny, golden, and hollow-sounding when tapped. Turn out on to a wire rack to cool.

Pain Amuse-gueule
(Flavoured Brioche)
• Make one quantity Brioche dough up to step 7, adding 250g (8oz) diced Gruyère, 1 tablespoon each dried *herbes de Provence*, dried mint, and dried oregano, and 1 teaspoon each caraway seeds, coriander seeds, and fennel seeds to the dough with the softened butter in step 5.
• Replace the ten small brioche moulds with a buttered 1kg (2lb) loaf tin in step 6. Shape the dough for a tin loaf (*see page 53*).
• Put the dough in the prepared tin. Cover with a tea towel and prove until the dough rises to 1cm (¼in) below the top of the tin, about 45 minutes. Preheat the oven to 200°C/400°F/gas 6.
• Brush with the egg glaze and sprinkle with an additional 2 tablespoons grated Gruyère.
• Bake for 35 minutes until golden and hollow-sounding when tapped underneath. Turn out of the tin on to a wire rack to cool.

— HANDY TIPS —
• *Use the best-quality butter and freshest eggs available to make the most flavourful Brioche.*

• *Be sure that the eggs are at room temperature and the butter has been left out of the refrigerator to soften before starting.*

• *It is important to always use softened, not melted, butter to grease the brioche moulds.*

• *Use leftover Brioche to make luxurious Pain Perdu or a scrumptious Bread and Butter Pudding (see pages 158–159).*

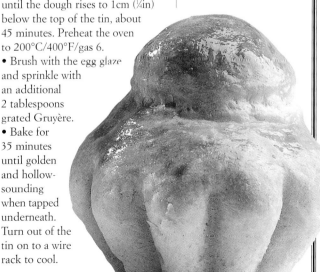

MANTOVANA
OLIVE OIL BREAD FROM MANTUA

This long loaf with a delicate, crispy crust and fine crumb takes its name, Mantovana, *from Mantua in Lombardy, Italy. The double rising produces a light, even texture. Be careful not to over-rise the bread – it might collapse when placed in a hot oven; do not leave the dough for any longer than 40 minutes for its second rising. Serve with sliced Parma ham or country salami.*

USING A BREAD MACHINE

If your machine has a programme for double rising, this bread may be made entirely in a machine. Follow the manufacturer's instructions (see pages 66–67).

INGREDIENTS

2 tsp dried yeast

600ml (1 pint) water

175g (6oz) wholemeal flour

500g (1lb) strong white flour

2 tsp salt

125ml (4fl oz) olive oil

1 Sprinkle the yeast into 400ml (14fl oz) of the water in a bowl. Leave for 5 minutes; stir to dissolve. Mix the flours together in a large bowl. Make a well in the centre and pour in the yeasted water.

2 Use a wooden spoon to draw enough of the flour into the yeasted water to form a soft paste. Cover the bowl with a tea towel, then leave to "sponge" until frothy and risen, about 20 minutes.

3 Add the salt and oil to the sponge. Mix in the rest of the flour from the sides of the well. Stir in the remaining water, as needed, to form a very sticky dough.

4 Turn the dough out on to a floured work surface. Knead until smooth, about 10 minutes.

5 Put the dough in a clean, oiled bowl and cover with a tea towel. Leave to rise until doubled in size, 50 minutes. Knock back, cover with a tea towel, and leave to rise until doubled in size again, 40 minutes.

6 Knock back and chafe for 10 minutes (see page 51), then leave to rest for 10 minutes.

7 Divide the dough into two pieces. Shape each piece into a long loaf (see page 52), about 25cm (10in) in length. Place on a floured baking sheet and cover with a tea towel. Leave to prove for 15 minutes.

8 Cut a 1cm (½in) deep, lengthways slash down the centre of each loaf (see page 62). Bake in the preheated oven for 45 minutes until golden and hollow-sounding when tapped underneath. Leave to cool on a wire rack.

To begin
Sponge method
Time: 20 minutes
(see page 44)

Rising
1½ hours
(see pages 50–51)

Proving
15 minutes
(see page 57)

Oven temperature
200°C/400°F/gas 6

Baking
45 minutes

Yield
2 loaves

Yeast alternative
15g (½oz)
fresh yeast
(see page 41)

PANE DI RAMERINO
ROSEMARY RAISIN BREAD

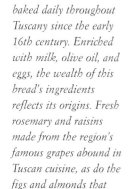

Quite simply the best accompaniment to fresh goat's cheese, and a superlative breakfast bread, too. This bread recipe is a Florentine speciality that has been baked daily throughout Tuscany since the early 16th century. Enriched with milk, olive oil, and eggs, the wealth of this bread's ingredients reflects its origins. Fresh rosemary and raisins made from the region's famous grapes abound in Tuscan cuisine, as do the figs and almonds that inspired this recipe's delicious variation.

USING A BREAD MACHINE
Unless you wish to hand-shape this bread, it may be made entirely in a machine. Follow the manufacturer's instructions (see pages 66–67).

INGREDIENTS
2 tsp dried yeast

100ml (3½fl oz) water

500g (1lb) strong white flour

1½ tsp salt

2 tbsp milk powder

1 tbsp fresh rosemary, chopped

250g (8oz) raisins

4 tbsp olive oil

4 eggs, beaten

1 Sprinkle the yeast into the water in a bowl. Leave for 5 minutes; stir to dissolve. Mix the flour, salt, and milk powder in a large mixing bowl. Make a well in the centre and add the yeasted water and all the remaining ingredients.

2 Mix the flour into the yeast mixture to form a soft, sticky dough. Add extra flour, 1 tablespoon at a time, if the dough is too moist.

3 Turn the dough out on to a lightly floured work surface. Knead until silky, springy, and elastic, about 10 minutes.

4 Put the dough in a clean, oiled bowl and cover with a tea towel. Leave to rise until doubled in size, about 2 hours. Knock back and chafe for 5 minutes (*see page 51*), then leave to rest for 10 minutes.

5 Divide the dough into two pieces. Shape each into a round loaf (*see page 54*).

Place on two oiled baking sheets and cover with tea towels. Leave to prove until doubled in size, about 1 hour. These loaves will spread and look slightly flat after rising, but they will rise up dramatically during the initial stages of baking.

6 Cut a slash 1cm (½in) deep across the top of each loaf, then another in the opposite direction to make an "X" (*see page 62*).

7 Bake in the preheated oven for 45 minutes until golden brown and hollow-sounding when tapped underneath. Cool on a wire rack.

VARIATION
Pane ai Fichi con Mandorle (Fig Bread with Almonds)
• Make one quantity Panmarino dough up to step 7, replacing the fresh rosemary with 125g (2oz) whole almonds, toasted and chopped, the raisins for the same amount of finely chopped dried figs, and the olive oil for the same amount of orange juice. Preheat the oven to 200°C/400°F/gas 6.
• Bake as directed in step 7. Sieve with a generous dusting of icing sugar over the top before serving.

 Rising
2 hours
(*see pages 50–51*)

 Proving
1 hour
(*see page 57*)

 Oven temperature
200°C/400°F/gas 6

 Baking
45 minutes

 Yield
2 loaves

 Yeast alternative
15g (½oz)
fresh yeast
(*see page 41*)

TORTA DI TESTA DI PROSCIUTTO E FORMAGGIO
GOLDEN CHEESE AND HAM BREAD

This lovely golden loaf, marbled with savoury morsels of ham and cheese, makes a perfect accompaniment – fresh, warm, or toasted – to a bowl of hot soup. It also makes a delicious base for the ultimate toasted cheese sandwich.

USING A BREAD MACHINE
This bread may be made entirely in a machine. Follow the manufacturer's instructions (see pages 66–67).

INGREDIENTS
2 tsp dried yeast

100ml (3½fl oz) water

500g (1lb) strong white flour

1½ tsp salt

¼ tsp freshly ground black pepper

a pinch of freshly grated nutmeg

125g (4oz) unsalted butter, softened

4 eggs, beaten

150g (5oz) sliced prosciutto, chopped

150g (5oz) Emmental, diced

oil, to grease baking sheet

1 Sprinkle the yeast into the water in a bowl. Leave for 5 minutes; stir to dissolve. Mix the flour, salt, pepper, and nutmeg together in a large bowl. Make a well in the centre and pour in the yeasted water, butter, eggs, prosciutto, and cheese.

2 Mix the flour from the sides of the well into the yeasted water to form a soft, sticky dough.

3 Turn out on to a lightly floured work surface. Knead until silky and elastic, about 10 minutes.

4 Put the dough in a clean bowl and cover with a tea towel. Leave to rise until doubled in size, about 2 hours. Knock back, then leave to rest for a further 10 minutes.

5 Shape the dough into a round loaf (*see page 54*). Place on a lightly oiled baking sheet and cover with a tea towel. Leave to prove until doubled in size, about 1 hour.

6 Bake in the preheated oven for 1½ hours until golden brown. Leave to cool on a wire rack.

 Rising
2 hours
(*see pages 50–51*)

 Proving
1 hour
(*see page 57*)

 Oven temperature
180°C/350°F/gas 4

 Baking
1½ hours

 Yield
1 loaf

 Yeast alternative
15g (½oz)
fresh yeast
(*see page 41*)

TORTA DI TESTA DI PROSCIUTTO E FORMAGGIO

ZOPF

SWISS PLAITED LOAF

This shiny, golden milk loaf is made throughout Switzerland but is said to have originated in the Emmental region, where it is called Zupfe. *The bread, enriched with the sweet butter and creamy milk of the region, then braided and baked to a glossy gold, is a traditional part of the annual thanksgiving meal in honour of the Emmentaler harvest. It is also very popular breakfast fare all over Switzerland, especially on New Year's Day morning.*

USING A BREAD MACHINE

Use the dough setting (see pages 66–67). Remove the dough after rising and follow steps 6–8.

INGREDIENTS

2 tsp dried yeast

300ml (½ pint) milk

500g (1lb) strong white flour

1½ tsp salt

60g (2oz) unsalted butter, softened and creamed, plus extra to grease baking sheet

1 tsp granulated sugar

2 tbsp kirsch or brandy

egg glaze, made with 1 egg yolk and 1 tbsp milk (see page 58)

1 Sprinkle the yeast into 100ml (3½fl oz) of the milk in a bowl. Leave for 5 minutes; stir to dissolve. Put the flour in a large bowl. Make a well in the centre and pour in the yeasted milk.

2 Use a wooden spoon to draw enough of the flour into the yeasted milk to form a soft paste. Cover the bowl with a tea towel, then leave to "sponge" until frothy and risen, about 20 minutes.

3 Pour the remaining milk, holding back about half, into the well. Mix in the flour. Add to it the salt, butter, sugar, and kirsch. Stir in the reserved milk, as needed, to form a soft, moist dough.

4 Turn the dough out on to a lightly floured work surface.

Knead until smooth, shiny, and elastic, about 10 minutes.

5 Put the dough in a clean bowl and cover with a tea towel. Leave to rise until doubled in size, about 1½–2 hours. Knock back, then rest for 10 minutes.

6 Divide the dough into three pieces. Roll out each piece to form a 40cm (16in) long rope and make a plaited loaf (*see page 57*).

7 Place on a buttered baking sheet and cover with a tea towel. Prove until doubled in size, about 35–45 minutes. Brush the top of the loaf with the egg glaze.

8 Bake in the preheated oven for 40 minutes until golden brown and hollow-sounding when tapped underneath. Cool on a wire rack.

VARIATION
Pain Viennois (Vienna Bread)

• Make one quantity Zopf dough up to step 5, excluding the sugar and kirsch added in step 3.
• Divide the dough into two equal-sized pieces, then shape each piece into an oval loaf (*see page 55*).
• Place on a buttered baking tray and cover with a tea towel.
• Leave to prove until doubled in size, about 1½–2 hours. Preheat the oven to 180°C/350°F/gas 4.
• Brush with the egg glaze. Cut ten diagonal slashes, about 5mm (¼in) deep, along the length of each loaf (*see page 62*).
• Bake for 35–45 minutes. Leave to cool on a wire rack.

To begin
Sponge method
Time: 20 minutes
(*see page 44*)

Rising
1½–2 hours
(*see pages 50–51*)

Proving
35–45 minutes
(*see page 57*)

Oven temperature
180°C/350°F/gas 4

Baking
40 minutes

Yield
1 loaf

Yeast alternative
15g (½oz)
fresh yeast
(*see page 41*)

ZOPF

PARKER HOUSE ROLLS

The Parker House Roll originated in the Parker House Hotel in Boston. A butter-and-egg enriched dough is cut into small rectangles, brushed with melted butter, folded in half, and baked until soft and golden brown. Serve these dangerously moreish rolls warm – allow to cool on a wire rack for 10 minutes, then wrap in a clean cloth to keep them warm.

USING A BREAD MACHINE

Use the dough setting (see pages 66–67). Remove the dough after rising and follow steps 5–7.

INGREDIENTS

2½ tsp dried yeast

250ml (8fl oz) milk

60g (2oz) unsalted butter, melted

30g (1oz) melted butter, to glaze, plus extra to grease bowl and baking sheet

2 tbsp granulated sugar

2 eggs, beaten

560g (1lb 2oz) strong white flour

2 tsp salt

1 Sprinkle the yeast into 100ml (3½fl oz) of the milk in a bowl. Leave for 5 minutes; stir to dissolve. Warm the remaining milk in a saucepan with the butter and sugar. Stir continuously, until the butter has melted. Cool until tepid, then beat in the eggs until evenly combined.

2 Mix the flour and salt together in a large bowl. Make a well in the centre and pour in the yeasted milk and the butter mixture. Mix in the flour to form a soft, sticky dough.

3 Turn the dough out on to a floured work surface. Knead until smooth, shiny, and elastic, about 10 minutes. Knead in extra flour, 1 tablespoon at a time, if the dough is too sticky. Resist adding too much flour – the dough should not be dry, but soft.

4 Put the dough in a buttered bowl and cover with a tea towel. Leave to rise until doubled in size, 1–1½ hours.

5 Knock back, then leave to rest for 10 minutes. Divide the dough into two pieces. Roll out each piece to form a 20cm x 40cm (8in x 16in) rectangle. Cut each rectangle lengthways into four strips, each 5cm (2in) wide. Cut each strip into four rectangles, each 10cm (4in) long. Brush half of each rectangle with melted butter, then fold in half, leaving a 1cm (½in) flap.

6 Place the rolls on a buttered baking sheet so that each roll overlaps slightly with the one next to it; cover with a tea towel. Prove until doubled in size, about 30 minutes.

7 Brush the tops of the rolls with melted butter. Bake in the preheated oven for 15–20 minutes until golden and hollow-sounding when tapped underneath. Leave to cool on a wire rack.

 Rising
1–1½ hours
(see pages 50–51)

 Proving
30 minutes
(see page 57)

 Oven temperature
220°C/425°F/gas 7

 Baking
15–20 minutes

 Yield
16 rolls

 Yeast alternative
20g (¾oz)
fresh yeast
(see page 41)

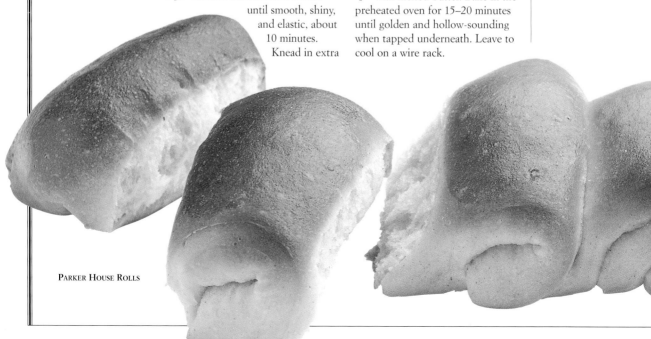

PARKER HOUSE ROLLS

BOW KNOT ROLL

VARIATIONS

Soft Dinner Rolls

• Make one quantity Parker House Rolls dough up to step 5.

• Divide the dough into 16 pieces. Shape each piece of dough into a round roll (*see page 55*).

• Arrange the rolls 5cm (2in) apart on two buttered baking sheets. Cover with a tea towel and prove until doubled in size, 30 minutes.

• Brush each roll with an egg glaze, made with 1 egg yolk and 1 tablespoon milk. Preheat the oven to 220°C/425°F/gas 7.

• Bake for 15–20 minutes until golden. Leave to cool on a wire rack.

Snail Rolls

• Make one quantity Parker House Rolls dough up to step 5.

• Divide the dough into 16 pieces. Roll each piece into a 30cm (12in) rope and form into a coil, tucking under the end (*see left*).

• Place on two buttered baking sheets and prove as instructed for Soft Dinner Rolls. Preheat the oven to 220°C/425°F/gas 7.

• Top the rolls as you prefer (*see pages 58–61*). Bake for 15–20 minutes until golden. Leave to cool on a wire rack.

Baker's Knot Rolls

• Make one quantity Parker House Rolls dough up to step 5.

• Divide the dough into 16 pieces. Roll each

piece into a 30cm (12in) rope, then shape into a figure of eight and tuck the ends through the holes.

• Place on two buttered baking sheets and prove as instructed for Soft Dinner Rolls. Preheat the oven to 220°C/425°F/gas 7.

• Glaze and top the rolls as you prefer (*see pages 58–61*). Bake for 15–20 minutes. Cool on a wire rack.

Bow Knot Rolls

• Make one quantity Parker House Rolls dough up to step 5.

• Divide into 16 pieces. Shape each piece into a knot roll (*see page 55*).

• Place on two buttered baking sheets and prove as instructed for Soft Dinner Rolls. Preheat the oven to 220°C/425°F/gas 7.

• Glaze and top the rolls as you prefer (*see pages 58–61*). Bake for 15–20 minutes. Cool on a wire rack.

SNAIL ROLL

Cloverleaf Rolls

• Make one quantity Parker House Rolls dough up to step 5.

• Divide into 16 pieces. Divide each piece into three even portions. Shape each piece into a round roll (*see page 55*). Place three balls in each buttered cup of a muffin tin.

• Leave to prove until doubled in size, about 30 minutes. Preheat the oven to 220°C/425°F/gas 7.

• Glaze and top the rolls as you prefer (*see pages 58–61*). Bake for 15–20 minutes. Cool on a wire rack.

CLOVERLEAF ROLL

TWIST ROLL

Twist Rolls

• Make one quantity Parker House Rolls dough up to step 5.

• Divide the dough into 16 pieces. Roll each piece of dough into a 30cm (12in) rope, fold in half, and twist; pinch the ends to seal.

• Place on two buttered baking sheets and prove as instructed for Soft Dinner Rolls. Preheat the oven to 220°C/425°F/gas 7.

• Glaze and top the rolls as you prefer (*see pages 58–61*). Bake for 15–20 minutes.

SHAPING A SNAIL ROLL

Roll each piece of dough into a 30cm (12in) rope. Form each rope into a coil, tucking the end underneath.

PARTYBROT
GERMAN PARTY BREAD

This German party bread makes a decorative centrepiece at any occasion. Classic dinner rolls are baked together in a round cake tin and may be sprinkled with the topping of your choice (see pages 60–61).

USING A BREAD MACHINE
Use the dough setting (see pages 66–67). Remove the dough after rising and follow steps 2–6.

INGREDIENTS
1 quantity dough
(see Parker House Rolls, page 118)

unsalted butter, melted, to grease tin

for the topping

egg glaze, made with 1 egg yolk and 1 tbsp milk (see page 58)

1 tbsp each sesame seeds and poppy seeds

1 Make the dough as directed in the recipe for Parker House Rolls (*see page 118*) up to step 5.

2 Knock back, then leave to rest for 10 minutes. Divide into 19 equal-sized pieces. Shape each piece into a round, smooth ball (*see page 55*). Grease a round cake tin or spring form pan, about 24cm (9½in) in diameter, with the melted butter.

3 Arrange the shaped rolls in the prepared tin by making an outer ring of 12 rolls, and an inner ring of six rolls, and placing the last roll in the centre of the two rings.

4 Cover the tin with a tea towel, then leave to prove until the rolls double in size, about 45 minutes.

5 **To make the topping** Brush the top of each roll with the egg glaze, and sprinkle alternately with the sesame and poppy seeds.

6 Bake in the preheated oven for 45 minutes until golden and hollow-sounding when tapped. Turn out on to a wire rack to cool slightly, then wrap in a tea towel to keep warm. Serve immediately.

 Rising
1–1½ hours
(*see pages 50–51*)

 **Proving**
45 minutes
(*see page 57*)

 Oven temperature
200°C/400°F/gas 6

 Baking
45 minutes

 Yield
19 rolls

 Yeast alternative
15g (½oz)
fresh yeast
(*see page 41*)

FAN TANS
DECORATIVE BUTTERMILK ROLLS

These pretty, dainty rolls make perfect party fare. A speciality of New England, they are sometimes called Yankee Buttermilk Rolls. If you do not have any buttermilk in the house refer to the glossary on page 64 for a suggested substitution. The fancy shape of the rolls is easy to replicate when you follow the illustrated steps at the bottom of the page.

USING A BREAD MACHINE
Use the dough setting (see pages 66–67). Remove the dough after rising and follow steps 4–7.

INGREDIENTS
2 tsp dried yeast

½ tsp granulated sugar

200ml (7fl oz) buttermilk

375g (13oz) strong white flour

½ tsp baking soda

½ tsp salt

60g (2oz) unsalted butter, melted, plus extra to grease tin

1 Sprinkle the yeast and sugar into the buttermilk in a bowl. Leave for 5 minutes; stir to dissolve. Mix the flour, baking soda, and salt in a large bowl. Make a well in the centre and pour in the yeasted buttermilk and 30g (1oz) of the melted butter.

2 Mix in the flour to form a soft, moist dough. Turn the dough out on to a lightly floured work surface. Knead until smooth, glossy, and elastic, about 10 minutes.

3 Put the dough in a clean bowl and cover with a tea towel. Leave to rise until doubled in size, about 1–1½ hours.

4 Knock back, then leave to rest for 10 minutes. Roll out to form a rectangle, 50cm x 30cm x 2.5mm (20in x 12in x ⅛in). Brush with the remaining melted butter.

5 Use a sharp knife to cut the buttered dough into seven strips, each about 4cm (1¼in) wide. Place the strips in a stack, then cut the stack (see below, left).

6 Turn each piece cut-side up and pinch the underside together to seal. Place the rolls in a buttered muffin or bun tin (see below, right) and cover with a tea towel. Leave to prove until doubled in size, about 1 hour.

7 Bake in the preheated oven for 15–20 minutes until golden. Turn out on to a wire rack to cool slighty, then serve still warm.

Rising
1–1½ hours
(see pages 50–51)

Proving
1 hour
(see page 57)

Oven temperature
200°C/400°F/gas 6

Baking
15–20 minutes

Yield
8 rolls

Yeast alternative
15g (½oz)
fresh yeast
(see page 41)

SHAPING THE ROLLS

In step 5, place the cut dough strips on top of one another to form an even stack. Use a sharp knife to cut the stack crossways into eight equal pieces.

In step 6, turn each piece cut-side up and pinch the underside together to seal. Place the shaped rolls, pinched side down, in a buttered muffin tin.

SWEDISH DILL BREAD

This bread is simply wonderful with smoked salmon. It has a moist crumb, a light texture subtly scented with dill, and a golden crust studded with toasted onion.

USING A BREAD MACHINE

This bread may be made entirely in a machine. Follow the manufacturer's instructions (see pages 66–67).

INGREDIENTS

2 tsp dried yeast

125ml (4fl oz) water

500g (1lb) strong white flour

1 tsp salt

2 tbsp chopped fresh dill

150g (5oz) cream cheese, at room temperature

2 onions, roughly chopped

30g (1oz) unsalted butter, softened, plus extra to grease tin

1 egg, beaten

1 Sprinkle the yeast into the water in a bowl. Leave for 5 minutes; stir to dissolve. Mix the flour and salt together in a large bowl.

2 Make a well in the centre and add the dill, cream cheese, onions, butter, egg, and yeasted water. Use a wooden spoon to mix all the ingredients together with the flour to form a stiff, sticky dough.

3 Turn the dough out on to a lightly floured work surface. Knead the dough until silky and elastic, about 10 minutes.

4 Put the dough in a clean bowl and cover with a tea towel. Leave the dough to rise until doubled in size, about 1½ hours.

5 Grease a 1kg (2lb) loaf tin with butter. Knock back the dough, then leave to rest for 10 minutes.

6 Shape the dough for a loaf tin (*see page 53*). Place seam-side down in the prepared tin and cover with a tea towel. Prove until the dough has risen 1cm (½in) above the top of the tin, about 1½ hours.

7 Bake in the preheated oven for 45 minutes–1 hour until deeply golden and hollow-sounding when tapped underneath. Turn out on to a wire rack and leave to cool.

Rising
1½ hours
(*see pages 50–51*)

Proving
1½ hours
(*see page 57*)

Oven temperature
180°C/350°F/gas 4

Baking
45 minutes–1 hour

Yield
1 loaf

Yeast alternative
15g (½oz) fresh yeast
(*see page 41*)

CINNAMON RAISIN BREAD

When sliced and toasted this bread is perhaps North America's favourite breakfast loaf – a great accompaniment to a full weekend breakfast of eggs, bacon, and freshly squeezed juice. Any leftover slices make the perfect ingredients for another weekend breakfast favourite – "French Toast" or Pain Perdu (see page 158).

USING A BREAD MACHINE

Use the dough setting (see pages 66–67). Remove the dough after rising and follow steps 6–9.

INGREDIENTS

90g (3oz) dark brown sugar

200ml (7fl oz) milk

2 tsp dried yeast

500g (1lb) strong white flour

1½ tsp salt

2 tsp ground cinnamon

2 eggs, beaten

3 tbsp unsalted butter, melted

150g (5oz) raisins

egg glaze, made with 1 egg yolk and 1 tbsp water (see page 58)

1 Add the dark brown sugar to 100ml (3½fl oz) of the milk in a bowl. Stir to dissolve completely. Sprinkle the yeast into the milk. Leave for 5 minutes; stir to dissolve.

2 Mix the flour, salt, and cinnamon together in a large bowl. Make a well in the centre and add the yeasted milk, beaten eggs, and melted butter.

3 Mix in the flour. Stir in the remaining milk, as needed, to form a moist, sticky dough.

4 Turn the dough out on to a lightly floured work surface. Knead until smooth, soft, and supple, about 10 minutes.

5 Put the dough in a clean bowl and cover with a tea towel. Leave the dough to rise until doubled in size, about 1–1½ hours.

6 Grease a 1kg (2lb) loaf tin with butter. Knock back the dough, then leave to rest for 10 minutes.

7 Roll out the dough on a lightly floured work surface to form a 20cm x 30cm (8in x 12in) rectangle. Sprinkle with the raisins, pressing them down lightly into the dough.

8 Roll the dough tightly like a Swiss roll. Pinch the seam to seal. Place in the loaf tin with the seam underneath (*see page 53*). Cover with a tea towel and leave to prove until the dough is 1cm (½in) above the top of the tin, 30–45 minutes.

9 Brush the loaf with the egg glaze and bake in the preheated oven for 45 minutes, then reduce the temperature to 180°C/350°F/gas 4 and bake for a further 30 minutes until dark, shiny, and hollow-sounding when tapped underneath. Turn out on to a wire rack and leave to cool.

 Rising
1–1½ hours
(*see pages 50–51*)

 Proving
30–45 minutes
(*see page 57*)

 Oven temperature
200°C/400°F/gas 6

 Baking
1¼ hours

 Yield
1 loaf

 Yeast alternative
15g (½oz)
fresh yeast
(*see page 41*)

PRUNE & CHOCOLATE BREAD

This deeply indulgent loaf, chock-a-block with juicy prunes and melted chocolate, is superlative served warm and cut into thick slices. The prunes and chocolate are best roughly chopped so that the bread is packed with large chunks of flavour. Try the Triple Chocolate and Hazelnut variation as a special treat for your favourite chocolate-lover.

USING A BREAD MACHINE

Use the dough setting (see page 66–67). Remove the dough after rising and follow steps 5–7.

INGREDIENTS

2½ tsp dried yeast

350ml (12fl oz) water

500g (1lb) strong white flour

1½ tsp salt

30g (1oz) unsalted butter, softened, plus extra to grease tin

200g (7oz) pitted prunes, roughly chopped

200g (7oz) plain chocolate, roughly chopped

1 egg, beaten

1 Sprinkle the yeast into 100ml (3½fl oz) of the water in a bowl. Leave for 5 minutes, then stir to dissolve. Mix the flour and salt together in a large bowl. Make a well in the centre of the flour and pour in the yeasted water.

2 Mix in the flour. Stir in the remaining water, as needed, to form a soft, sticky dough.

3 Turn the dough out on to a lightly floured work surface. Knead the dough until smooth and elastic, about 10 minutes.

4 Put the dough in a clean bowl and cover with a tea towel. Leave to rise until doubled in size, about 1 hour. Grease a 1kg (2lb) loaf tin with softened butter.

5 Knock back the dough, then leave to rest for 10 minutes. Add the prunes, chocolate, butter, and egg (*see below, left*). Turn out on to a lightly floured work surface. Knead until just firm enough to shape, 1–2 minutes.

6 Shape the dough for a loaf tin (*see below, right*) and place in the prepared tin. Cover with a tea towel and leave to prove until the dough has risen 2.5cm (1in) above the rim of the tin, about 30 minutes.

7 Bake in the preheated oven for 45 minutes until lightly browned and hollow-sounding when tapped underneath. Turn out on to a wire rack and leave to cool.

VARIATION
Triple Chocolate and Hazelnut Bread

• Make one quantity Prune and Chocolate Bread dough up to step 5.
• Replace the prunes and 200g (7oz) plain chocolate in step 5 with: 250g (8oz) plain chocolate, 125g (4oz) dark chocolate, 60g (2oz) milk chocolate, roughly chopped, and 125g (4oz) hazelnuts, toasted and roughly chopped. Add to the dough (*see below, left*).
• Shape, prove, and bake the dough as directed in steps 6 and 7.

 Rising
1 hours
(*see pages 50–51*)

 Proving
30 minutes
(*see page 57*)

 Oven temperature
180°C/350°F/gas 4

 Baking
45 minutes

 Yield
1 loaf

 Yeast alternative
20g (¼oz)
fresh yeast
(*see page 41*)

ENRICHING THE DOUGH

Use your hand to gently squeeze the prunes, chocolate, butter, and egg into the dough until they are evenly distributed and the beaten egg is absorbed.

SHAPING THE DOUGH

Follow the instructions on page 53 to gently shape the dough to fit the loaf tin. Place the dough into the buttered tin seam-side down.

FLAT BREADS

FLAT BREADS WERE UNDOUBTEDLY SOME OF THE EARLIEST BREADS EVER BAKED. THEY CONTINUE TO BE PRODUCED TODAY, OFTEN SERVING AS PLATES AND CUTLERY FOR MEALS IN THEIR COUNTRIES OF ORIGIN. THEY ARE STAPLES PARTICULARLY IN THOSE PARTS OF THE WORLD WHERE FUEL FOR COOKING IS SCARCE – FLAT BREADS COOK VERY QUICKLY. MANY OF THESE BREADS ARE SHAPED WITH A ROLLING PIN. BREAD DOUGH ROLLS OUT MOST EASILY WHEN RESTED AT INTERVALS. WHEN MAKING THESE RECIPES ROLL OUT THE DOUGH UNTIL YOU FEEL RESISTANCE, THEN TURN TO ANOTHER PIECE OF DOUGH, AND GIVE THE FIRST PIECE TIME TO REST. REPLICATE THE FIERCE HEAT OF THE CLAY OVENS TRADITIONALLY USED TO MAKE FLAT BREADS BY PREHEATING A HEAVY BAKING SHEET WHEN STATED IN THE RECIPES.

LEFT **NAAN BREADS WITH A VARIETY OF TOPPINGS**

NAAN
PUNJABI FLAT BREAD

This tear-drop-shaped, leavened flat bread originates in the Punjab region of northern India. Naan *are traditionally baked by slapping the dough on to the side of a hot, dome-shaped clay oven called a tandoor. The weight of the dough creates the characteristic tear-drop shape. An essential accompaniment to any classic tandoori meat or chicken dish, home-baked* Naan *are best eaten while still hot and fresh, with yogurt and Indian-style pickles and chutneys.*

USING A BREAD MACHINE
Use the dough setting (see pages 66–67). Remove the dough after rising and follow steps 5–7.

INGREDIENTS
2 tsp dried yeast

250ml (8fl oz) milk

500g (1lb) plain flour

1½ tsp salt

1 tsp granulated sugar

3 tbsp plain yogurt

30g (1oz) ghee or unsalted butter, melted

1 Sprinkle the yeast into 100ml (3½fl oz) of the milk in a bowl. Leave for 5 minutes; stir to dissolve. Mix the flour and salt together in a large bowl. Make a well in the centre and add the yeasted milk, sugar, yogurt, and ghee or butter.

2 Mix in the flour. Stir in the remaining milk, as needed, to form a stiff, sticky dough.

3 Turn the dough out on to a lightly floured work surface. Knead the dough until smooth, stiff, and elastic, about 10 minutes.

4 Put the dough in a clean bowl and cover with a tea towel. Leave to rise until doubled in size, about 3–4 hours.

5 Knock back, then leave to rest for 10 minutes. Divide into four equal pieces. On a lightly floured surface, roll out each piece to form a round, 15cm (6in) across and 5mm (¼in) thick. Pull one side to form a tear shape; stretch the dough until about 25cm (10in) long. Preheat the grill on the highest possible setting.

6 Preheat a baking sheet under the grill for about 2 minutes. Place a piece of dough on the hot baking sheet. Grill the dough in batches of two for about 2–3 minutes on each side, until puffy and golden.

7 Stack the grilled breads on top of each other and cover with a clean, dry cloth to keep the crusts soft and to prevent drying out.

VARIATIONS
Sada Naan
(Seeded Indian Flat Bread)
• Make one quantity Naan dough up to step 6.
• Combine 2 tablespoons poppy seeds and 1 tablespoon sesame seeds with 1 tablespoon softened butter.
• Spread each piece of dough with a layer of the seeded butter.
• Preheat the baking sheet and grill the breads as directed in steps 6–7.

Badami Naan
(Almond Indian Flat Bread)
• Make one quantity Naan dough up to step 6.
• Combine 60g (2oz) blanched, flaked almonds and 1 tablespoon sesame seeds in a bowl.
• Melt 1 tablespoon butter, then brush over each piece of shaped dough.
• Sprinkle the almonds and seeds evenly over each piece and press down lightly into the dough.
• Preheat the baking sheet and grill the breads as directed in steps 6–7.

Rising
3–4 hours
(*see pages 50–51*)

Cooking
4–6 minutes
per batch

Yield
4 breads

Yeast alternative
15g (½oz)
fresh yeast
(*see page 41*)

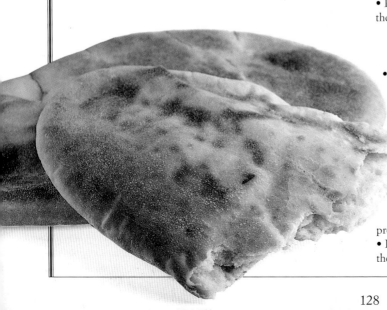

EKMEK

TURKISH COUNTRY BREAD

The Turks are great bread eaters and this is very much a daily staple. Flattened, ridged rounds are the most common form given to this dough, but other popular shapes include egg-glazed rings and decorative, plump plaits, liberally sprinkled with sesame seeds or poppy seeds. This soft, oil-enriched bread is an Eastern Mediterranean cousin of the Italian Focaccia. It is best eaten while still warm.

USING A BREAD MACHINE

Use the dough setting (see pages 66–67). Remove the dough after rising, brush it with oil, then follow steps 6–8.

INGREDIENTS

1 tsp runny honey

325ml (11fl oz) water

2 tsp dried yeast

500g (1lb) strong white flour

1½ tsp salt

2 tbsp olive oil, plus extra to coat and glaze

1 Stir the honey into 150ml (¼ pint) of the water in a bowl, then sprinkle in the yeast. Leave for 5 minutes, then stir to dissolve. Mix the flour and salt together in a large bowl. Make a well in the centre and pour in the yeasted liquid.

2 Use a wooden spoon to draw enough of the flour into the yeasted water to form a soft paste. Cover the bowl with a tea towel, then leave to "sponge" until frothy and risen, about 20 minutes.

3 Pour the remaining water, holding back about half, and the olive oil into the well. Mix in the flour. Stir in the reserved water, as needed, to form a firm, moist dough.

4 Turn the dough out on to a lightly floured work surface.

Knead until smooth, shiny, and elastic, about 10 minutes.

5 Put the dough in a well-oiled bowl, turning it to coat evenly with the oil; cover with a tea towel. Leave to rise until doubled in size, about 1½–2 hours.

6 Knock back, then leave to rest for 10 minutes. On a lightly floured work surface, use your hands to flatten the dough into a round, 23cm (9in) across and 2.5cm (1in) thick. Place on a floured baking sheet and cover with a tea towel. Leave to prove until doubled in size, about 45 minutes.

7 Brush the dough with olive oil. Use the blunt edge of a knife to make four parallel indentations across the dough, then four more indentations in the opposite direction to make a criss-cross pattern, leaving a 2.5cm (1in) border around the edge.

8 Bake in the preheated oven for 40 minutes until golden and hollow-sounding when tapped underneath. Sprinkle with extra oil, then leave to cool on a wire rack.

To begin
Sponge method
Time: 20 minutes
(*see page 44*)

Rising
1½–2 hours
(*see pages 50–51*)

Proving
45 minutes
(*see page 57*)

Oven temperature
220°C/425°F/gas 7

Baking
40 minutes

Yield
1 loaf

Yeast alternative
15g (½oz)
fresh yeast
(*see page 41*)

CARTA DA MUSICA
"MUSIC PAPER" BREAD

Called Carta da Musica, *"music paper", because of the crunchy sound it makes when broken, this light, thin flat bread is native to Sardinia. Once baked, it may be stored for several weeks. If you are ambitious, try splitting each baked round into two for an even thinner result. Remove the bread from the oven and cut an incision along one edge with a paring knife. Use your hands to separate the bread into two very thin rounds and return them to the oven on a baking tray to crispen for one minute.*

USING A BREAD MACHINE
Use the dough setting (see pages 66–67). Remove the dough after rising and follow steps 5–8.

INGREDIENTS

1¼ tsp dried yeast
325ml (11fl oz) water
500g (1lb) strong white flour
1½ tsp salt

1 Sprinkle the yeast into the water in a bowl. Leave for 5 minutes, then stir to dissolve.

2 Mix the flour and salt together in a large bowl. Make a well in the centre and pour in the yeasted water. Mix in the flour from the sides to form a stiff, sticky dough.

3 Turn the dough out on to a lightly floured work surface. Knead the dough until smooth and elastic, about 10 minutes.

4 Put the dough in a clean bowl and cover with a tea towel. Leave to rise for just 20 minutes.

5 Lightly flour a baking sheet and place it in the preheated oven for 5–10 minutes. Divide the dough into 16 equal-sized pieces. On a lightly floured work surface, roll out the first piece of dough to form a paper-thin round, 16cm (6in) across (*see below, left*).

6 Cover the remaining pieces of dough with a damp tea towel to prevent them from drying out. If the dough resists shaping, cover it with a damp tea towel and leave it to rest for 2 minutes. While the first piece rests, begin rolling out the next piece.

7 Immediately place the rolled out dough on the preheated, floured baking sheet (*see below, right*). Bake in the preheated oven for about 10 minutes, turning the risen round over once, until lightly coloured and puffy. Reflour the baking sheet; repeat with each shaped dough round.

8 Remove the breads from the oven and pile them on top of one another on a wire rack. Leave to cool; as the breads cool they will become crisp and brittle.

Rising
20 minutes
(*see pages 50–51*)

Oven temperature
200°C/400°F/gas 6

Baking
10 minutes
per bread

Yield
16 breads

Yeast alternative
10g (⅓oz)
fresh yeast
(*see page 41*)

ROLLING OUT THE DOUGH

In step 5, use a narrow, floured rolling pin to roll out each piece of the dough into a paper-thin round. Cover with a damp tea towel and rest the dough for 2 minutes if it resists rolling out.

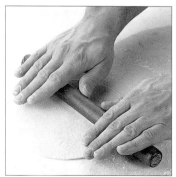

In step 7, lift the dough from the work surface with the rolling pin and transfer it to a preheated, floured baking sheet.

PIADINA
ITALIAN FLAT BREAD

PIADINA FILLED WITH PROSCIUTTO AND BASIL

Once the everyday fare of the Romagna region, this rustic flat bread is now popular all over Italy, especially in bars, where it is usually served warm. It is either eaten as an antipasto, *cut into wedges and sprinkled with olive oil and salt, or as a* panini, *wrapped around the filling of your choice, such as prosciutto and basil (see above).*

USING A BREAD MACHINE
Use the dough setting (see pages 66–67). Remove the dough after rising and follow steps 5–8.

INGREDIENTS

2 tsp dried yeast
75ml (2½fl oz) water
500g (1lb) strong white flour
2 tsp salt
1 tbsp olive oil
250ml (8fl oz) carbonated water

1 Sprinkle the yeast into the water in a bowl. Leave for 5 minutes; stir to dissolve. Mix the flour and salt together in a large bowl. Make a well in the centre and pour in the yeasted water, the oil, and 150ml (¼ pint) of the carbonated water.

2 Mix in the flour. Stir in the reserved carbonated water, as needed, to form a firm, moist dough.

3 Turn the dough out on to a lightly floured work surface. Knead until smooth, shiny, and elastic, about 10 minutes.

4 Put the dough in a clean bowl and cover with a tea towel. Leave to rise until doubled in size, about 1½ hours. Knock back, then leave to rest for a further 10 minutes.

5 Divide the dough into eight equal-sized pieces. On a lightly floured work surface, roll out each piece to form a round, 15cm (6in) across and 1cm (½in) thick. If the dough resists rolling out, leave it to rest for 1–2 minutes, then continue.

6 Heat a heavy frying pan or griddle over a medium-low heat until very hot, about 10 minutes.

7 Place one of the dough rounds in the hot pan and prick all over with a fork to prevent air bubbles. Cook until golden brown on both sides, flipping it over frequently to avoid scorching and to aid even cooking, about 5 minutes.

8 Repeat with the remaining dough rounds as directed in step 7. Stack the rounds on top of each other and cover with a tea towel to keep soft and warm.

Rising
1½ hours
(see pages 50–51)

Cooking
5 minutes
per bread

Yield
8 breads

Yeast alternative
15g (½oz)
fresh yeast
(see page 41)

TORTA AL TESTO
"BREAD OF THE TILE"

The appearance of this age-old peasant bread inspired its name – testo meaning "tile" in Italian. Torta al Testo is found almost exclusively in its native Umbria, and then usually "a casa" (in the home). It is usually cooled, sliced, stacked, and wrapped in foil, then filled and reheated just before serving.

USING A BREAD MACHINE

Use the dough setting (see pages 66–67). Remove the dough after rising and follow steps 5–9.

INGREDIENTS
for the dough

2 tsp dried yeast

315ml (10½fl oz) water

500g (1lb) strong white flour

1½ tsp salt

1 tbsp olive oil

for the filling

250g (8oz) fontina

125g (4oz) rocket leaves

salt and freshly ground pepper

1 Sprinkle the yeast into 200ml (7fl oz) of the water in a bowl. Leave for 5 minutes, then stir to dissolve. Mix the flour and salt together in a large bowl. Make a well in the centre and pour in the yeasted water and the olive oil.

2 Mix in the flour, and stir in the reserved water, as needed, to form a firm, moist dough.

3 Turn the dough out on to a lightly floured work surface. Knead until smooth, shiny, and elastic, about 10 minutes.

4 Put the dough in a clean bowl and cover with a tea towel. Leave to rise until doubled in size, about 30 minutes.

5 Knock back, then leave to rest for 10 minutes. Divide into eight pieces. On a lightly floured work surface, roll out each piece of dough to form a round, 20cm (8in) across and 5mm (¼in) thick. If the dough resists rolling out, leave it to rest for 1–2 minutes, then continue.

6 Heat a heavy frying pan or griddle over a medium-low heat until very hot, about 10 minutes.

7 Place one of the dough rounds in the hot pan and prick all over with a fork to prevent air bubbles. Cook until golden on both sides, flipping it over frequently to avoid scorching and to aid even cooking, about 5 minutes. Repeat with the remaining dough rounds.

8 Stack the rounds on top of each other and cover with a tea towel to keep soft and warm. When cool enough to handle, use a sharp knife to cut around the edge of each bread and, using your hands, separate it into two halves. Top one half of with fontina and rocket, and season with salt and pepper.

9 Place the other half on top of the filling and place the stuffed breads on two baking sheets. Bake in the preheated oven for 5 minutes until hot and the cheese has melted. Cut into wedges. Serve immediately.

 Rising
30 minutes
(see pages 50–51)

 Oven temperature
180°C/350°F/gas 4

 Cooking
5 minutes per bread, plus 5 minutes

 Yield
8 breads

 Yeast alternative
15g (½oz) fresh yeast *(see page 41)*

PITTA
MIDDLE EASTERN BREAD POUCH

The staple bread of the Middle East, called Khubz in Arabic, this is more commonly known by its Greek name of Pitta in the West. Its soft, chewy crust, absorbent crumb, and hollow pouch make it the most versatile of breads, ideal to scoop up, dip in, wrap around, or be filled with all manner of food. Best served warm, Pitta can be easily reheated: sprinkle lightly with water and warm in the oven. Keep Pitta in a sealed plastic bag to prevent dryness.

USING A BREAD MACHINE
Use the dough setting (see pages 66–67). Remove the dough after rising, brush it with oil, then follow steps 5–7.

INGREDIENTS

2 tsp dried yeast

½ tsp granulated sugar

300ml (½ pint) water

500g (1lb) strong white flour

1 tsp salt

2 tbsp olive oil, plus extra to coat

1 Sprinkle the yeast and sugar into 100ml (3½fl oz) of the water in a bowl. Leave for 5 minutes; stir to dissolve. Mix the flour and salt together in a large bowl. Make a well in the centre and pour in the yeasted liquid and the olive oil.

2 Mix in the flour. Stir in the remaining water, as needed, to form a firm but soft dough.

3 Turn the dough out on to a lightly floured work surface. Knead until smooth, supple, and elastic, about 15 minutes. Initially, the dough will be quite stiff. It will soften and stretch gradually as you continue kneading.

4 Put the dough in an oiled bowl, turning it to coat evenly with the oil, then cover with a tea towel. Leave to rise until doubled in size, about 1½ hours.

5 Knock back, then leave to rest for 10 minutes. Divide the dough into eight pieces. Shape each piece into a smooth ball (*see page 55*). On a lightly floured work surface, roll out each ball to form an oval, 22cm (9in) long and 5mm (¼in) thick.

6 Cover with a tea towel and leave to prove until slightly risen, about 20 minutes.

7 Dust two baking sheets with flour and preheat in the oven for 5 minutes. Place the dough ovals on the hot baking sheets and return immediately to the oven. Bake for 5–10 minutes until puffy. Wrap in a clean, dry cloth to keep the crusts soft and to prevent drying out.

VARIATIONS
Wholemeal Pitta

- Make one quantity Pitta dough up to step 3, replacing the strong white flour with 125g (4oz) strong wholemeal flour and 375g (13oz) strong white flour.
- Continue with the recipe as directed in steps 3–7.

Lavash
(Armenian Flat Bread)
(see page 22 for illustration)

- Make one quantity Pitta dough up to step 5.
- Divide the dough into eight pieces. Shape each piece into a smooth ball (*see page 55*). Roll out each piece of dough on a lightly floured work surface to form a very thin round, about 30cm (12cm) across.
- If the dough resists rolling out, leave it to rest for 1–2 minutes, then continue. Cover the dough with a tea towel and leave to prove for 20 minutes. Preheat the oven to 220°C/425°F/gas 7.
- Dust two baking sheets with flour and preheat in the oven for 5 minutes. Bake the shaped dough pieces for 2–5 minutes per batch until puffy and lightly coloured.
- Wrap in a clean, dry cloth to keep the crusts soft and to prevent the breads from drying out.

Rising
1½ hours
(*see pages 50–51*)

Proving
20 minutes
(*see page 57*)

Oven temperature
220°C/425°F/gas 7

Baking
5–10 minutes

Yield
8 breads

Yeast alternative
15g (½oz)
fresh yeast
(*see page 41*)

PAIN TUNISIEN

TUNISIAN SEMOLINA AND OLIVE OIL BREAD

This golden, seeded bread is made with fine semolina, ground from North African durum wheat, which is also used to make couscous, the staple grain of the region. The soft, absorbent crumb is especially suited to soaking up the rich, spicy sauces of tagines, the full-flavoured, slow-simmered stews of northern Africa. This bread is perhaps best enjoyed as the heart of a simple meal, served with a bowl of olives, a few dates, and a plate of cubed white cheese.

USING A BREAD MACHINE

Use the dough setting (see pages 66–67). Remove the dough after rising and follow steps 5–8.

INGREDIENTS

2 tsp dried yeast

175ml (6fl oz) water

250g (8oz) semolina

250g (8oz) strong white flour

1½ tsp salt

125ml (4fl oz) olive oil

egg glaze, made with 1 egg yolk and 1 tbsp water (see page 58)

4 tbsp sesame seeds

1 Sprinkle the yeast into 100ml (3½fl oz) of the water in a bowl. Leave for 5 minutes; stir to dissolve. Mix the semolina, flour, and salt together in a large bowl. Make a well in the centre and pour in the yeasted liquid and the olive oil.

2 Mix in the flour. Stir in the remaining water, as needed, to form a stiff, sticky dough.

3 Turn out on to a floured work surface. Knead the dough until smooth and elastic, about 10 minutes.

4 Put the dough in a clean, oiled bowl and cover with a tea towel. Leave to rise until doubled in size, about 1–1½ hours.

5 Knock back, then leave to rest for 10 minutes. Divide the dough into two pieces. On a lightly floured work surface, shape each piece into a flattened round, 18cm (7in) across and 2.5cm (1in) thick.

6 Place the dough rounds on oiled baking sheets, then cover with a tea towel. Leave to prove until doubled in size, about 30–45 minutes.

7 Brush the tops of the dough rounds with the egg glaze and sprinkle evenly with sesame seeds. Prick all over with a skewer or toothpick to prevent air bubbles.

8 Bake in the preheated oven for 30 minutes until golden brown and hollow-sounding when tapped underneath. Cool on a wire rack.

Rising
1–1½ hours
(see pages 50–51)

Proving
30–45 minutes
(see page 57)

Oven temperature
200°C/400°F/gas 6

Baking
30 minutes
Steam optional
(see page 63)

Yield
2 loaves

Yeast alternative
15g (½oz)
fresh yeast
(see page 41)

BARBARI
PERSIAN SESAME BREAD

INGREDIENTS

1 tsp runny honey

325ml (11fl oz) water

2 tsp dried yeast

500g (1lb) strong white flour

1½ tsp salt

2 tbsp olive oil, plus extra to glaze

2 tsp sesame seeds

This light, crusty bread is Iran's favourite breakfast bread, especially when topped with crumbled white cheese and sprinkled with fresh herbs. When made with milk instead of water and sprinkled with sugar instead of sesame seeds, the bread is called Shirmal *and is a much loved children's snack.*

USING A BREAD MACHINE

Use the dough setting (see pages 66–67). Remove the dough after rising, brush it with oil, then follow steps 6–9.

1 Stir the honey into 175ml (6fl oz) of the water in a bowl, then sprinkle in the yeast. Leave for 5 minutes; stir to dissolve. Mix the flour and salt together in a large bowl. Make a well in the centre and pour in the yeasted mixture.

2 Use a wooden spoon to draw enough of the flour into the yeasted mixture to form a soft paste. Cover the bowl with a tea towel, then leave to "sponge" until frothy and risen, about 20 minutes.

3 Pour the remaining water, holding back about half, and the olive oil into the well. Mix in the rest of the flour. Stir in the reserved water, as needed, to form a firm, moist dough.

4 Turn the dough out on to a lightly floured work surface. Knead until smooth, shiny, and elastic, about 10 minutes.

5 Put the dough in a clean, oiled bowl, turning it to coat evenly with the oil, then cover with a tea towel. Leave to rise until doubled in size, about 1½–2 hours.

6 Knock back, then leave to rest for 10 minutes. Divide into four equal pieces. Shape each piece into a round 12cm (5in) across and 2.5cm (1in) thick. Cover with a tea towel and leave to prove until doubled in size, about 45 minutes.

7 Dust two baking sheets with flour and preheat in the oven until very hot, about 15 minutes.

8 Use your fingertips to gently press into the surface of the dough to form nine dimples, about 2cm (¾in) deep, across the top of each round. Brush each round with olive oil and sprinkle with sesame seeds.

9 Place the shaped dough on the hot baking sheets and bake in the preheated oven for 20 minutes until golden brown and hollow-sounding when tapped underneath. Leave to cool on a wire rack.

VARIATION
Spicy Seeded Persian Bread
• Make one quantity Barbari dough up to step 8, mixing 1 teaspoon paprika and ¼ teaspoon cayenne pepper into the flour in step 1.
• In step 8, dimple each round as instructed in the recipe.
• Brush the rounds with olive oil, then sprinkle 2 teaspoons each sesame seeds, poppy seeds, and cumin seeds evenly over the top of the four rounds.
• Preheat the oven to 220°C/425°F/ gas 7. Place the shaped dough on the hot baking sheets and bake in the preheated oven for 20 minutes until golden and hollow-sounding when tapped underneath. Cool on a wire rack.

To begin
Sponge method
Time: 20 minutes
(*see page 44*)

Rising
1½–2 hours
(*see pages 50–51*)

Proving
45 minutes
(*see page 57*)

Oven temperature
220°C/425°F/gas 7

Baking
20 minutes

Yield
4 breads

Yeast alternative
15g (½oz)
fresh yeast
(*see page 41*)

PIDE

TURKISH SEEDED BREAD POUCH

Pide *is baked in great quantities during the holy month of Ramadan. According to the Koran, bread was sent down to earth by God's command, and this soft, seeded bread is traditionally eaten at sundown to break the daily fast. Plain* Pide *is an accompaniment to grilled kebabs and* Köfte.

USING A BREAD MACHINE

Use the dough setting (see pages 66–67). Remove the dough after rising, brush it with oil, then follow steps 6–9.

INGREDIENTS

2 tsp dried yeast

½ tsp granulated sugar

325ml (11fl oz) water

500g (1lb) strong white flour

1 tsp salt

2 tbsp olive oil

egg glaze, made with 1 egg and 1 tbsp water (see page 58)

2 tsp nigella seeds

1 Sprinkle the yeast and sugar into 125ml (4fl oz) of the water in a bowl. Leave for 5 minutes, then stir to dissolve.

2 Sift the flour and salt together in a large bowl. Make a well in the centre and pour in the yeasted water and the olive oil.

3 Mix in the flour. Stir in the remaining water, as needed, to form a firm but soft dough.

PIDE

4 Turn the dough out on to a lightly floured work surface. Knead until smooth, supple, and elastic, about 15 minutes. Initially, the dough will be quite stiff. It will soften and stretch gradually as you continue kneading.

5 Put the dough in a clean, oiled bowl, turning it to coat evenly with the oil. Cover with a tea towel, then leave to rise until doubled in size, about 1½ hours.

6 Knock back, then leave to rest for 10 minutes. Divide into two equal-sized pieces. Roll each piece into a smooth ball (*see page 55*). On a lightly floured work surface, roll out each piece of dough to form a round 25cm (10in) across, and 5mm (¼in) thick. Cover with a tea towel and leave to prove for 20 minutes.

7 Use the blunt edge of a knife to gently draw four parallel impressions across the top of each dough round, then four more impressions across the top in the opposite direction, to make a criss-cross pattern. Brush the rounds with the egg glaze.

8 Sprinkle the dough rounds evenly with nigella seeds, then place them on lightly floured baking sheets.

9 Bake in the preheated oven for 10–15 minutes until puffy and lightly coloured. Wrap the breads immediately in a tea towel to keep the crusts soft and to prevent drying out.

 Rising
1½ hours
(*see pages 50–51*)

 Proving
20 minutes
(*see page 57*)

 Oven temperature
220°C/425°F/gas 7

 Baking
10–15 minutes
Steam optional
(*see page 63*)

 Yield
2 breads

 Yeast alternative
15g (½oz)
fresh yeast
(*see page 41*)

QUICK BREADS

QUICK BREADS CAN BE MADE IN MINUTES SINCE THEY DO NOT REQUIRE THE PROLONGED KNEADING AND LENGTHY RISING ESSENTIAL FOR YEAST-LEAVENED BREADS. INSTEAD OF YEAST, THESE BREADS ARE MADE WITH A CHEMICAL RAISING AGENT SUCH AS BAKING POWDER OR BAKING SODA. THESE RELEASE GAS BUBBLES THE MOMENT IT IS MOISTENED. WHEN MAKING QUICK BREADS BLEND THE WET AND DRY INGREDIENTS SEPARATELY AND COMBINE THEM JUST BEFORE BAKING. SWIFT, GENTLE MIXING IS ESSENTIAL BECAUSE IF THE BATTER IS BEATEN TOO VIGOROUSLY, THE GLUTEN IN THE FLOUR WILL STRENGTHEN THE MIXTURE AND THE THE LOAF WILL BE TOUGH. QUICK BREADS ARE NOT SUITABLE FOR MAKING IN BREAD MACHINES.

LEFT **QUICK BREAD MUFFINS IN A VARIETY OF FLAVOUR VARIATIONS**

CRANBERRY NUT LOAF

Cranberries give this festive, fruity, quick bread a juicy, tart bite that offsets the sweet, cakey crumb. This recipe can be adapted to make muffins as well as many other flavoured loaves.

USING A BREAD MACHINE

This recipe is not suitable for bread machines.

INGREDIENTS

1 tbsp oil, to grease tin

250g (8oz) plain flour, plus extra to dust tin

1½ tsp baking powder

½ tsp baking soda

½ tsp salt

60g (2oz) pecans, coarsely chopped

1 egg, beaten

175ml (6fl oz) milk

150g (5oz) granulated sugar

60g (2oz) unsalted butter, melted

175g (6oz) cranberries

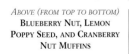

ABOVE (FROM TOP TO BOTTOM)
BLUEBERRY NUT, LEMON POPPY SEED, AND CRANBERRY NUT MUFFINS

1 Grease a 1kg (2lb) loaf tin with oil. Generously dust with flour, then turn the tin to coat the bottom and sides evenly. Shake out any excess flour.

2 Sift the flour, baking powder, baking soda, and salt together in a large bowl. Stir in the pecans and make a well in the centre. Put the remaining ingredients in a separate bowl and mix until thoroughly combined.

3 Pour the liquid mixture and the cranberries into the flour well. Use a spatula to gently fold all the ingredients together to form a wet batter. (Over mixing can result in a heavy bread.)

4 Spoon the batter into the prepared loaf tin. Bake in the preheated oven for 1 hour until golden and well-risen. The bread is ready when the edges shrink from the sides of the tin, and a metal skewer inserted into the centre comes out clean.

5 Keep the bread in the tin and leave to stand, about 10 minutes. Carefully run a knife around the edges and turn out. Cool on a wire rack.

VARIATIONS

Jamaican Banana Bread

• Make one quantity Cranberry Nut Loaf batter, replacing the cranberries with three ripe bananas (350g/12oz), peeled and mashed, in step 2.

• Add ½ teaspoon ground cinnamon and ¼ teaspoon ground nutmeg to the batter in step 3.

• Spoon the batter into the prepared loaf tin, and decorate the top with 30g (1oz) pecan halves.

• Bake and cool as directed in steps 4–5 of the main recipe.

Cranberry Nut Muffins

• Make one quantity Cranberry Nut Loaf batter up to step 4. Grease eight holes of a 12-hole muffin tin with oil. Preheat the oven to 180°C/350°F/gas 4.

• Spoon the batter into the muffin tin, dividing it equally between the greased holes. Bake for 15 minutes.

• Remove from the oven and allow to stand, about 10 minutes. Run a knife around the edges of the baked muffins to loosen them. Turn out, and leave to cool on a wire rack.

Blueberry Nut Muffins

• Make one quantity Cranberry Nut Loaf batter up to step 4, replacing the cranberries with 175g (6oz) fresh blueberries in step 2.

• Spoon the batter into the prepared tin as directed in the recipe for Cranberry Nut Muffins.

• Bake and cool as directed in the recipe for Cranberry Nut Muffins.

Lemon Poppy Seed Muffins

• Make one quantity Cranberry Nut Loaf batter up to step 4, replacing the cranberries and pecans with 2 tablespoons poppy seeds and the grated zest of one lemon in step 2.

• Spoon the batter into the prepared tin as directed in the recipe for Cranberry Nut Muffins.

• Bake and cool as directed in the recipe for Cranberry Nut Muffins.

 Oven temperature
180°C/350°F/gas 4

Baking
1 hour

Yield
1 loaf

AUSTRALIAN DAMPER BREAD

Early Australian settlers named this bread damper for its "dampening", or filling effect on the appetite. Originally made just from plain flour mixed with water, kneaded into a round, flat cake, it was baked in the ashes of a camp fire. Salt, milk, butter, and baking powder were added when, and if, they were available.

USING A BREAD MACHINE
This recipe is not suitable for bread machines.

INGREDIENTS
375g (13oz) strong white flour

125g (4oz) wholemeal flour

4 tsp baking powder

1 tsp salt

375ml (13fl oz) milk, plus extra, to glaze

30g (1oz) unsalted butter, melted

1 Sift the flours, baking powder, and salt together in a large bowl. Make a well in the centre of the flour mixture.

2 Stir the milk and the melted butter together in a separate bowl. Pour the milk-butter mixture into the flour well and mix quickly to form a soft, sticky dough.

3 Turn the dough out on to a lightly floured work surface. Knead the dough lightly until smooth and soft, about 1 minute.

4 Shape into a round loaf (*see page 54*) and place on a buttered baking sheet. Brush with milk and sprinkle with wholemeal flour.

5 Cut a slash (*see page 62*), 2cm (1in) deep, across the top of the loaf, then another in the opposite direction to make an "X".

6 Bake in the preheated oven for 15 minutes, then reduce the temperature to 180°C/350°F/gas 4 and bake for a further for 25 minutes until golden and hollow-sounding when tapped. Cool on a wire rack.

Oven temperature
220°C/425°F/gas 7

Baking
40 minutes

Yield
1 loaf

IRISH SODA BREAD

In Ireland, many traditional baked goods, from soda bread to scones, are made with buttermilk – the liquid left over from churning butter. If you have problems finding buttermilk, simply substitute soured milk: place 1 tablespoon of lemon juice or cider vinegar in a measuring jug and fill it up to the 300ml (½ pint) mark with ordinary milk. This bread is best eaten on the day it is baked.

USING A BREAD MACHINE
This recipe is not suitable for bread machines.

INGREDIENTS
250g (8oz) plain flour, plus extra, to dust

250g (8oz) wholemeal flour

1 tsp baking soda

1 tsp salt

30g (1oz) unsalted butter

300ml (½ pint) buttermilk

1 Sift the flours, baking soda, and salt together in a large bowl. Rub the butter into the flour with your fingertips until evenly dispersed.

2 Make a well in the centre of the mixture and pour in the buttermilk. Use a wooden spoon to stir in the flour to form a soft, crumbly dough.

3 Turn out on to a lightly floured work surface. Knead the dough very lightly until smooth, silky, and elastic, about 3 minutes.

4 Shape into a flattened round about 15cm (6in) across and 5cm (2in) thick. Dust with flour. Cut a slash (*see page 62*), 2cm (1in) deep, across the top, then another in the opposite direction to make an "X".

5 Bake in the preheated oven for about 35 minutes until hollow-sounding when tapped underneath. Cover with a cloth, then leave to cool on a wire rack.

Oven temperature
200°C/400°F/gas 6

Baking
35 minutes
Steam optional
(*see page 63*)

Yield
1 loaf

CLASSIC CORN BREAD

Corn bread is the original all-American bread. Recipes vary from family to family and region to region, some made using white corn, others with yellow, some thin, others well-risen. This version has an airy, slightly crunchy texture.

USING A BREAD MACHINE
This recipe is not suitable for bread machines.

INGREDIENTS
30g (1oz) unsalted butter, melted, plus extra, to grease tin

150g (5oz) fine cornmeal or maize meal

150g (5oz) plain flour

2 tsp baking powder

½ tsp baking soda

1 tbsp caster or granulated sugar

½ tsp salt

2 eggs, beaten

150ml (¼ pint) buttermilk

150ml (¼ pint) milk

1 Grease a 23cm (9in) square, 5cm (2in) deep, metal tin with melted butter. Place in the preheated oven, until very hot.

2 Stir the cornmeal, flour, baking powder, baking soda, sugar, and salt together in a large bowl until thoroughly combined. Make a well in the centre. Whisk the eggs, buttermilk, and milk together in a separate bowl and stir in the melted butter.

3 Pour the mixture into the well, then use a spatula to gently fold all the ingredients together to form a wet batter. (Over mixing can result in a heavy bread.)

4 Spoon the batter into the hot, buttered tin – it should sizzle. Bake in the preheated oven for 20–25 minutes until golden and well-risen. It is ready when the edges shrink from the sides of the tin and a metal skewer inserted into the centre comes out clean.

5 Turn out of the tin and leave to cool slightly on a wire rack. Cut into squares and serve warm.

VARIATIONS
Corn Sticks
(see page 21 for illustration)
Corn sticks require a special cast-iron pan with moulds shaped like little ears of corn *(see page 36)*.
• Preheat the oven to 220°C/425°F/gas 7. Grease the pan with oil, ensuring that the moulds are thoroughly coated. Place in the oven, and leave until very hot.
• Make one quantity Classic Corn Bread batter as directed in steps 2–3.
• Grease the pan again with melted butter, and spoon the batter into the moulds until just full.
• Bake for 15–20 minutes until golden and the edges shrink from the sides of the tin.
• Gently ease out the sticks with a wooden skewer. Quickly re-butter the mould and bake the second batch. Serve hot or warm.

Tex-Mex Skillet Corn Bread
(see opposite for illustration)
• Preheat the oven to 220°C/425°F/gas 7. Prepare a 23cm (9in), heavy, cast-iron skillet according to the instructions given for the cast-iron corn stick mould above.
• Make one quantity Corn Bread batter as directed up to step 4. Stir 125g (4oz) grated Cheddar then 2 jalapeño chillies, deseeded and chopped, into the batter in step 3.
• Spoon the batter into the prepared skillet and bake for 20–25 minutes until golden and well-risen. Turn out and leave to cool slightly on a wire rack. Cut into wedges and serve warm.

Oven temperature
220°C/425°F/gas 7

Baking
20–25 minutes

Yield
1 loaf

PAIN D'EPICE
FRENCH HONEY-SPICE BREAD

This aromatic bread dates from medieval times. It improves on keeping: for best results cool the bread in baking parchment, double wrap in foil, and store at room temperature for up to three days before eating.

USING A BREAD MACHINE
This recipe is not suitable for bread machines.

INGREDIENTS

1 tbsp oil, to grease tin

350ml (12fl oz) runny honey

40g (1½oz) dark brown sugar

125g (4oz) wholemeal flour

125g (4oz) rye flour

2 tsp baking powder

½ tsp ground cinnamon

½ tsp ground anise seeds

¼ tsp each ground star anise, grated nutmeg, ground cloves, ground ginger

zest of 1 orange, grated

2 eggs, beaten

100ml (3½fl oz) milk

1 Grease a 1kg (2lb) loaf tin with oil and line the sides and bottom of the tin with baking parchment. Put the honey and the sugar in a pan over a low heat and stir until viscous, about 3 minutes.

2 Sift the flours, baking powder, spices, and orange zest together in a large bowl. Make a well in the centre and pour in the eggs and milk.

3 Stir in the honey mixture, drawing in the flour to form a smooth batter. Pour the batter into the tin; it will be three-quarters full.

4 Bake in the preheated oven for 1¼ hours until dark and fragrant. Owing to its high sugar content, the loaf may need to be covered with foil to prevent burning, since the top will become very dark during cooking. The bread is ready when a metal skewer inserted into the centre comes out clean. Turn out of the loaf tin, and leave to cool on a wire rack.

Oven temperature
220°C/425°F/gas 7

Baking
1¼ hours

Yield
1 loaf

OLD ENGLISH CHEESE & APPLE LOAF

This moist and flavourful loaf, with its superlatively crunchy, cheesy crust, is perfect picnic and tea-time fare. Any apples you have on hand will do for this recipe, however crisp, sharp cooking apples like Granny Smith or Bramley are preferred.

USING A BREAD MACHINE
This recipe is not suitable for bread machines.

INGREDIENTS

1 tbsp oil, to grease tin

500g (1lb) plain flour

1 tbsp baking powder

½ tsp salt

60g (2oz) unsalted butter

4 apples, peeled, cored, and grated

125g (4oz) Cheddar, grated

2 eggs, beaten

rolled porridge oats, to sprinkle

1 Grease a 1kg (2lb) loaf tin with oil. Sift the flour, baking powder, and salt together in a large bowl.

2 Rub the butter into the flour mixture swiftly with your fingertips until the flour mixture resembles the texture of coarse breadcrumbs throughout.

3 Stir the grated apple and cheese into the flour and butter mixture. Add the beaten eggs and mix everything together until thoroughly blended.

4 Spoon the batter into the prepared tin and sprinkle the top with oats. Bake in the preheated oven for 1½–2 hours until golden brown and well-risen. The bread is ready when a metal skewer inserted into the centre comes out clean. Turn out of the loaf tin and leave to cool on a wire rack.

Oven temperature
180°C/350°F/gas 4

Baking
1½–2 hours

Yield
1 loaf

NUTTY YOGURT BREAD

Any well-stocked larder will furnish the ingredients for this useful all-purpose emergency loaf. Quick and easy to make, this crusty loaf studded with crunchy nuts and seeds is a perfect accompaniment to a bowl of steaming soup. Delicious when served warm from the oven, it also toasts exceptionally well.

USING A BREAD MACHINE

This recipe is not suitable for bread machines.

INGREDIENTS

1 tbsp sunflower oil, plus extra to grease tin

375g (13oz) plain flour

125g (4oz) wholemeal flour

1 tsp salt

1 tsp cream of tartar

1 tsp baking soda

1 tsp baking powder

90g (3oz) mixed nuts, chopped

90g (3oz) sunflower seeds

1 tsp runny honey

200ml (7fl oz) plain yogurt

300ml (½ pint) milk

2 tbsp sunflower seeds, for sprinkling

1 Grease a 1kg (2lb) loaf tin with oil. Sift the flours, salt, cream of tartar, baking soda, and baking powder together in a large bowl. Stir in the nuts and sunflower seeds.

2 Mix the honey, yogurt, milk, and oil together. Stir into the dry ingredients and mix to form a soft dough.

3 Spoon the batter into the prepared tin and smooth to level the top. Sprinkle with sunflower seeds. Bake in the preheated oven for 1 hour until golden and risen. The bread is ready when its edges shrink from the sides of the tin.

VARIATIONS

Seeded Yogurt Bread
• Make one quantity Nutty Yogurt Bread batter as directed in steps 1–2, replacing the nuts and sunflower seeds with 3 tablespoons each sesame and poppy seeds.

• Continue as directed in step 3. Sprinkle the top of the loaf with 2 teaspoons each sesame and poppy seeds in place of the sunflower seeds.

Herbed Yogurt Bread
• Make one quantity Nutty Yogurt Bread batter as directed in steps 1–2, replacing the nuts and seeds with 2 teaspoons dried mixed herbs (preferably *herbes de Provence*).
• Continue as directed in step 3. Sprinkle the top of the loaf with 3 tablespoons grated Cheddar in place of the sunflower seeds.

Oaten Yogurt Bread
• Make one quantity Nutty Yogurt Bread batter as directed in steps 1–2, replacing the plain flour with the same amount of medium oatmeal and omitting the nuts and seeds.
• Continue as directed in step 3. Sprinkle the top of the loaf with 2 tablespoons rolled porridge oats in place of the sunflower seeds.

 Oven temperature 180°C/350°F/gas 4

 Baking 1 hour

 Yield 1 loaf

FESTIVE
BREADS

TRADITIONALLY, FESTIVE BREADS HAVE
PLAYED A CENTRAL ROLE IN RELIGIOUS
FEAST DAYS AND SEASONAL CELEBRATIONS.
AS A MARK OF THEIR SPECIAL, FESTIVE STATUS,
THESE BREADS ARE HEAVILY ENRICHED AND
HIGHLY FLAVOURED WITH ONCE-TREASURED
INGREDIENTS, SUCH AS FRESH EGGS AND BUTTER,
CANDIED FRUIT, SAFFRON, AND EXOTIC SPICES.
MADE WITH CARE FOR SPECIAL OCCASIONS, THE
RECIPES ARE OFTEN TIME-CONSUMING AND
ELABORATE TO PREPARE. A KNOWLEDGE OF THE
TECHNIQUES DISCUSSED IN THE FLAVOURED AND
ENRICHED BREAD SECTIONS, SUCH AS WORKING
IN HEAVY INGREDIENTS AND HANDLING SOFT,
BUTTER-AND-EGG-RICH DOUGHS, IS PARTICULARLY
USEFUL WHEN MAKING THESE BREADS.

LEFT **STOLLEN, THE TRADITIONAL
GERMAN CHRISTMAS BREAD**

DRESDNER CHRISTSTOLLEN
CHRISTMAS STOLLEN

A *speciality of Dresden, this traditional German Christmas bread is now enjoyed around the world. The name,* Christstollen, *meaning Christ-cake, is taken from its special shape – a long loaf with a ridge down the middle and tapering ends – which is said to represent the Christ Child wrapped in swaddling clothes. This rich, heavy fruit dough needs an extra-large amount of yeast to make it rise.*

USING A BREAD MACHINE
Use the dough setting (see pages 66–67). Remove the dough after rising and follow steps 5–8.

INGREDIENTS
200g (7oz) raisins

100g (3½oz) dried currants

100g (3½oz) mixed candied peel, chopped

100g (3½oz) blanched almonds, chopped

zest of 2 lemons, grated

½ tsp ground cardamom

¼ tsp freshly grated nutmeg

a pinch of black pepper

½ tsp vanilla extract

3 tbsp dark rum

6 tsp dried yeast

250ml (8fl oz) tepid milk

500g (1lb) strong white flour

1½ tsp salt

100g (3½oz) granulated sugar

150g (5oz) unsalted butter, softened

icing sugar, for dusting

1 Place the dried fruits, peel, nuts, lemon zest, spices and pepper in a bowl. Pour over the vanilla extract and rum, then leave to soak, 2 hours.

2 Sprinkle the yeast into the milk in a bowl. Leave for 5 minutes; stir to dissolve. Mix the flour and salt together in a large mixing bowl. Make a well in the centre of the flour and pour in the yeasted milk.

3 Use a wooden spoon to draw enough of the flour into the yeasted water to form a soft paste. Cover with a tea towel, and leave to "sponge" until frothy and risen, about 20 minutes. Add the sugar and butter to the flour well. Mix in the flour to form a soft, firm dough.

4 Turn the dough out on to a lightly floured work surface. Knead until smooth and elastic, about 10 minutes. Put the dough in a buttered bowl and cover with a tea towel. Leave to rise until doubled in size, about 1½ hours.

5 Knock back, then leave to rest for 10 minutes. On a lightly floured work surface, use the palms of both hands to flatten the dough into a square, about 2.5cm (1in) thick. Scatter the fruit and almond mixture evenly over the dough and knead gently until evenly incorporated (*see page 99*).

6 Roll the dough out on a lightly floured work surface to form a flat oval, 35cm (14in) long and 2.5cm (1in) thick. Place on a buttered baking sheet. Make a lengthways indentation down the centre. Fold the dough in half lengthways, leaving a 2.5cm (1in) flap. Press the flap over to seal.

7 Use your hands to plump a small, rounded ridge down the centre. Cover with a tea towel, and prove until doubled in size, about 1 hour.

8 Bake in the preheated oven for 1½ hours until firm, and a metal skewer inserted into the centre comes out clean. Leave to cool on a wire rack. Dust with icing sugar, then store in an airtight container for at least one week. Serve sliced.

To begin
Sponge method
Time: 20 minutes
(*see page 44*)

Rising
1½ hours
(*see pages 50–51*)

Proving
1 hour
(*see page 57*)

Oven temperature
180°C/350°F/gas 4

Baking
1½ hours

Yield
1 loaf

Yeast alternative
50g (1¼oz) fresh yeast
(*see page 41*)

FOUGASSE

PROVENÇAL HEARTH BREAD

This branch-shaped bread is the centrepiece of the famous 13 desserts of Provence that are traditional to the region's *Reveillon (Christmas Eve)* celebrations. After Midnight Mass, families return home for a glass of *vin chaud and a selection of 12 fruits, nuts, and sweetmeats arranged around the* Fougasse.

USING A BREAD MACHINE

Use the dough setting (see pages 66–67). Remove the dough after rising, brush it with oil, then follow steps 6–9.

SHAPING THE DOUGH

Use your fingers to open out each slash by gently pulling the dough apart at each end.

INGREDIENTS

2 tsp dried yeast

300ml (10fl oz) water

500g (1lb) strong white flour

1½ tsp salt

2 tbsp granulated sugar

1 tsp anise seeds

75ml (2½fl oz) olive oil

1 tbsp orange flower water

1 Sprinkle the yeast into 200ml (7fl oz) of the water in a bowl. Leave for 5 minutes; stir to dissolve. Mix the flour, salt, sugar, and anise seeds together in a large bowl. Make a well in the centre of the mixture, then pour in the yeasted water.

2 Use a wooden spoon to draw enough of the flour into the yeasted water to form a soft paste. Cover the bowl with a tea towel and leave the paste to "sponge" until frothy and risen, about 20 minutes.

3 Add the oil and orange flower water to the flour well. Mix in the flour. Stir in the remaining water, as needed, to form a soft dough.

4 Turn the dough out on to a lightly floured work surface. Knead until smooth and elastic, about 10 minutes.

5 Put the dough in a clean, oiled bowl, turning it to coat evenly with the oil, then cover it with a tea towel. Leave to rise until doubled in size, about 1½ hours.

6 Knock back, then leave to rest for 10 minutes. Divide the dough into two pieces. On a lightly floured work surface, use the palms of your hands to flatten each piece into a tear-shape, about 35cm (14in) long and 1.5cm (¼in) thick. If the dough resists shaping, leave it to rest for 1–2 minutes, then continue.

7 Put the shaped dough on two oiled baking sheets. To form the dough into a leaf shape, make three diagonal slashes across each piece of the dough (*see page 62*). Open out each slash gently (*see below, left*).

8 Cover the shaped dough, then leave to prove until an imprint of your finger springs back slowly (*see page 57*), about 45 minutes.

9 Bake in the preheated oven for 40–45 minutes until crisp, golden brown, and hollow-sounding when gently tapped underneath.

VARIATION
Fougasse aux Herbes
(Fougasse with Herbs)
• Make the dough as directed up to step 3, replacing the sugar, anise seeds, and orange flower water with 1 tablespoon *herbes de Provence*.
• Continue as directed in steps 3–9.

 To begin
Sponge method
Time: 20 minutes
(*see page 44*)

 Rising
1½ hours
(*see pages 50–51*)

 Proving
45 minutes
(*see page 57*)

 Oven temperature
180°C/350°F/gas 4

 Baking
40–45 minutes

 Yield
2 loaves

 Yeast alternative
15g (½oz)
fresh yeast
(*see page 41*)

CHALLAH
JEWISH SABBATH BREAD

Egg-enriched Challah (meaning "offering" in Hebrew) is usually a plaited loaf. It is the traditional Jewish Festival and Sabbath bread: the three braids symbolize truth, peace, and justice, while the poppy seed topping signifies the manna that fell from heaven. A coiled loaf is baked for the Jewish New Year celebrations of Rosh Hashanah, and its round shape symbolizes continuity since it has no beginning and no end.

USING A BREAD MACHINE
Use the dough setting (see pages 66–67). Remove the dough after rising, brush it with butter, then follow steps 5–7.

COILED CHALLAH

INGREDIENTS
2 tsp dried yeast

200ml (7fl oz) water

500g (1lb) strong white flour

½ tsp salt

2 tbsp runny honey

2 eggs, beaten

60g (2oz) unsalted butter, melted

egg glaze, made with 1 egg yolk beaten with 1 tbsp water (see page 58)

2 tsp poppy seeds, to decorate

1 Sprinkle the yeast into the water in a bowl. Leave for 5 minutes; stir to dissolve. Mix the flour and salt together in a bowl. Make a well in the centre and pour in the yeasted water.

2 Use a wooden spoon to draw enough of the flour into the yeasted water to form a soft paste. Cover the bowl with a tea towel then leave to "sponge" until frothy and risen, about 20 minutes.

3 Add the honey, beaten eggs, and melted butter to the flour well. Mix in the flour from the sides to form a soft dough. Turn the dough out on to a lightly floured surface. Knead until smooth, shiny, and elastic, about 10 minutes.

4 Put the dough in a buttered bowl, turning to coat evenly with the butter. Cover with a tea towel. Leave to rise until doubled in size, about 2 hours.

5 Knock back, then rest for 10 minutes. Divide into three equal pieces. Roll out each piece to form a 40cm (16in) long rope. Use the flattened palms of your hands to taper the ends of

each rope, so that it is thinner at both ends than in the middle, then plait the ropes (*see page 57*).

6 Place on a buttered baking sheet and cover with a tea towel. Prove until doubled in size, about 45 minutes–1 hour.

7 Brush with the egg glaze and sprinkle with poppy seeds. Bake in the preheated oven for 45 minutes until richly golden and hollow-sounding when tapped underneath. Cool on a wire rack.

VARIATIONS
Coiled Challah
• Make one quantity Challah dough up to step 5.
• Shape the dough into a long loaf (*see page 52*). Roll the dough under the palms of your hands, with even pressure, until it forms a rope, about 50cm (20in) long. Taper the ends.
• Coil the tapered rope into a "snail"-like spiral. Pinch the end of the coiled rope to seal.
• Continue as steps 6–7.

Pulla
(Finnish Crown Loaf)
(see page 18 for illustration)
• Infuse ¼ teaspoon saffron strands in 200ml (7fl oz) heated milk.
• Make one quantity Challah dough as directed in steps 1–3, replacing the water with the milk in step 1, the honey with 60g (2oz) caster sugar in step 3, and adding ½ teaspoon ground cardamom to flavour the dough in step 3.
• Continue as directed in step 4. Shape the dough to plait, as directed in step 5, but do not taper the ends. Plait the ropes (*see page 57*).
• Place on a buttered baking sheet; bring the ends of the plait together to form a circle, and pinch to seal.
• Continue as directed in steps 6–7, omitting the poppy seeds.

To begin
Sponge method
Time: 20 minutes
(*see page 44*)

Rising
2 hours
(*see pages 50–51*)

Proving
45 minutes–1 hour
(*see page 57*)

Oven temperature
180°C/350°F/gas 4

Baking
45 minutes

Yield
1 loaf

Yeast alternative
15g (½oz)
fresh yeast
(*see page 41*)

PAN DE MUERTO
"BREAD OF THE DEAD"

The staple flour in Mexico is cornmeal. Pan de Muerto, *which is baked specially for the Mexican Day of the Dead festival that takes place on All Souls' Day, is made instead with highly prized wheat flour. The bread is flavoured with orange water and anise seeds and decorated with pieces of dough formed into the shapes of bones. The bread is taken to the cemetery with other gifts including the symbolic flowers of the dead, yellow marigolds.*

USING A BREAD MACHINE
Use the dough setting (see pages 66–67). Remove the dough after rising and follow steps 6–8.

INGREDIENTS

2 tsp dried yeast

4 tbsp water

500g (1lb) plain flour

1 tsp salt

6 eggs, beaten

125g (4oz) unsalted butter, melted

125g (4oz) sugar

2 tsp anise seeds

1 tbsp orange flower water

zest of 1 orange, grated

egg glaze, made with 1 egg yolk beaten with 1 tbsp water (see page 58)

granulated sugar, to decorate

1 Sprinkle the yeast into the water in a bowl. Leave for 5 minutes; stir to dissolve. Mix the flour and salt together in a large bowl. Make a well in the centre of the flour and pour in the yeasted water.

2 Use a wooden spoon to draw enough of the flour into the yeasted water to form a soft paste. Cover with a tea towel and leave to "sponge" until frothy, about 20 minutes.

3 Add the eggs, butter, sugar, anise seeds, orange flower water, and orange zest to the flour well. Mix in the flour from the sides to form a soft, sticky dough.

4 Turn out on to a lightly floured work surface. Knead until smooth and elastic, 10 minutes.

5 Put the dough in a clean, buttered bowl, turning it to coat evenly with the butter. Leave to rise until doubled in size, about 2 hours.

6 Divide the dough into two equal pieces, and pinch off a quarter of each piece. Divide one of these small quarter pieces into two equal pieces and shape each one into a ball, 2.5cm (1in) across. Divide the other small quarter piece into 14 equal pieces, and shape each of these pieces into a cylinder, 1cm (½in) thick. Shape each cylinder into a small bone (*see below*).

7 Shape the two remaining large pieces of dough into two round loaves (*see page 54*). Place on a buttered baking sheet and stick one of the small balls on top of each loaf. Arrange the bones to form four crosses on the sides of each loaf.

8 Cover the shaped loaves with a tea towel and leave to prove until risen, about 30 minutes. Brush the loaves with the egg glaze and sprinkle with sugar. Bake in the preheated oven for 35 minutes until golden and hollow-sounding when tapped underneath. Cool on a wire rack. Sprinkle with granulated sugar.

To begin
Sponge method
Time: 20 minutes
(*see page 44*)

Rising
2 hours
(*see pages 50–51*)

Proving
30 minutes
(*see page 57*)

Oven temperature
180°C/350°F/gas 4

Baking
35 minutes

Yield
2 loaves

Yeast alternative
15g (½oz)
fresh yeast
(*see page 41*)

CIAMBELLA MANDORLATA
RING-SHAPED EASTER BREAD WITH NUT BRITTLE

Decorated with crunchy-sweet nut and spice topping, this Italian Easter bread is originally from Bologna, one of the capital cities of the Emilia Romagna region. This traditional ring-shaped loaf is said to represent the unity of the family. It is now common to see the bread in Italian bakeries all the year round, and not just during the Easter holidays.

INGREDIENTS

2 tsp dried yeast

100ml (3½fl oz) tepid milk

600g (1¼lb) strong white flour

2 tsp salt

125g (4oz) granulated sugar

zest of 3 lemons, grated

125g (4oz) unsalted butter, softened

3 eggs, beaten

100ml (3½fl oz) water

for the topping

4 tsp ground cinnamon

3 tbsp granulated sugar

125g (4oz) blanched almonds, toasted and roughly chopped

1 egg yolk

1 Sprinkle the yeast into the milk in a small bowl. Leave for 5 minutes; stir to dissolve. Mix the flour, salt, sugar, and lemon zest together in a large bowl. Make a well in the centre of the mixture then add to it the butter, eggs, and the yeasted milk.

2 Mix in the flour from the sides of the well. Add the water, 1 tablespoon at a time as needed, to form a soft, sticky dough.

3 Turn the dough out on to a lightly floured work surface. Knead until smooth, springy, and elastic, about 10 minutes.

4 Put the dough in a clean bowl and cover. Leave to rise until doubled in size, about 4 hours.

5 Knock back the dough, then leave to rest, covered with a tea towel, for about 10 minutes.

6 Divide the dough into two equal pieces and roll each piece into a 40cm (16in) long rope. Twist the two dough ropes together.

7 Place the shaped dough rope on a buttered baking sheet. Shape it into a ring by bringing the two ends of the rope together. Pinch them to seal, and cover with a tea towel. Prove until doubled in size, about 1½ hours.

8 **To make the topping** Mix the cinnamon, sugar, almonds, and egg yolk together in a bowl. Use a rubber spatula to spread the mixture evenly over the top of the ring. Bake in the preheated oven for 45 minutes until golden and hollow-sounding when tapped underneath. Cool on a wire rack.

Rising
4 hours
(see pages 50–51)

Proving
1½ hours
(see page 57)

Oven temperature
220°C/400°F/gas 6

Baking
45 minutes

Yield
1 loaf

Yeast alternative
15g (½oz) fresh yeast
(see page 41)

USING A BREAD MACHINE
Use the dough setting (see pages 66–67). Remove the dough after rising and follow steps 5–8.

BOLO-REI

EPIPHANY BREAD

This bread is traditionally eaten in Portugal to celebrate the feast of the Epiphany – when the Three Kings arrived at Bethlehem.

USING A BREAD MACHINE

Use the dough setting (see pages 66–67). Remove the dough after rising and follow steps 6–8.

INGREDIENTS

100g (3½ oz) glacé citrus peel, chopped

50g (1½ oz) raisins

50g (1½ oz) pine nuts

100ml (3½ fl oz) port

2½ tsp dried yeast

100ml (3½ fl oz) water

500g (1lb) strong white flour

1½ tsp salt

100g (3½ oz) unsalted butter, softened

100g (3½ oz) caster sugar

zest of 1 lemon and 1 orange

3 eggs, beaten

a dried broad bean and a small present

for the topping

egg glaze, made with 1 egg yolk beaten with 1 tbsp water (see page 58)

10 glacé cherries

2 segments each glacé orange, lemon, and lime peel

lump sugar, crushed, to decorate

apricot jam, to glaze

1 Soak the glacé peel, raisins, and pine nuts in the port overnight. Sprinkle the yeast into the water in a bowl. Leave for 5 minutes; stir to dissolve. Mix the flour and salt together in a large bowl. Make a well in the centre and pour in the yeasted water.

2 Use a wooden spoon to draw enough of the flour into the yeasted water to form a soft paste. Cover the bowl with a tea towel. Leave to "sponge" until frothy and slightly risen, about 20 minutes.

3 Beat the butter with the sugar and lemon and orange zest together in a separate bowl until light and fluffy. Add the eggs, one at a time, and beat well after each addition. Add the mixture to the flour well, then mix in the flour from the sides to form a soft dough.

4 Turn the dough out on to a lightly floured work surface. Knead until soft, smooth, silky, and elastic, about 10 minutes. Knead in the peel, raisins, and pine nuts until evenly distributed (*see page 99*).

5 Put the dough in a clean bowl and cover with a tea towel. Leave to rise until doubled in size, about 2 hours.

6 Knock back, then leave to rest for 10 minutes. Shape into a *couronne* (*see page 56*), then place it on a buttered baking sheet. Wrap a dried broad bean and a trinket or small present separately in grease-proof paper. Insert both packages in the bottom of the shaped dough.

7 Cover the dough with a tea towel, and leave to prove until doubled in thickness, about 1 hour.

8 **To make the topping** Brush the dough with the egg glaze then decorate with the glacé fruit and the crushed sugar. Bake in a preheated oven for 45 minutes until golden. Warm the apricot jam in a saucepan over low heat until liquid, then brush the top and sides of the bread with it to glaze. Leave to cool on a wire rack.

To begin
Sponge method
Time: 20 minutes
(*see page 44*)

Rising
2 hours
(*see pages 50–51*)

Proving
1 hour
(*see page 57*)

Oven temperature
180°C/350°F/gas 4

Baking
45 minutes

Yield
1 loaf

Yeast alternative
20g (¾ oz)
fresh yeast
(*see page 41*)

PANETTONE
MILANESE CHRISTMAS BREAD

Once upon a time, a Milanese baker named Toni fell in love with a very beautiful woman who walked past his bakery every day. The baker, determined to create a magnificent bread to tempt her inside, laboured for six months and finally created a tall, domed loaf that lured her in. But when their eyes met, he fell out of love with her. However, his toils were not in vain; his new creation, called Pan di Toni *("Toni's bread") – eventually corrupted to* Panettone *– is now renowned throughout Italy and the rest of the world as a favourite gift, especially at Christmas.*

USING A BREAD MACHINE

Use the dough setting (see pages 66–67). Remove the dough after rising and follow steps 6–9.

INGREDIENTS

2½ tsp dried yeast

225ml (7½fl oz) tepid milk

350g (12oz) plain flour

½ tsp salt

115g (4oz) unsalted butter, softened

2 egg yolks

60g (2oz) caster sugar

75g (2½oz) candied citrus peel, chopped

50g (1½oz) sultanas

a pinch of nutmeg, grated

zest of 1 lemon and 1 orange, grated

1 tsp vanilla extract

egg glaze, made with 1 egg yolk beaten with water (see page 58)

icing sugar, to decorate

1 Sprinkle the yeast into the milk in a bowl. Leave for 5 minutes; stir to dissolve. Mix the flour and salt together in a large bowl. Make a well in the centre of the flour and pour in the yeasted milk.

2 Use a wooden spoon to draw enough of the flour into the yeasted milk to form a soft paste. Cover the bowl with a tea towel, and leave to "sponge" until frothy and risen, 20 minutes.

3 Mix in the flour from the sides of the well to form a stiff dough.

4 Turn the dough out on to a lightly floured work surface. Knead until smooth and elastic, about 10 minutes.

5 Put the dough in a bowl and cover with a tea towel. Leave to rise until doubled in size, about 1 hour.

6 Knock back; rest for 10 minutes. Grease a round mould, either a deep cake tin, or a small saucepan, about 20cm (8in) across and 15cm (6in) deep, with 15g (½oz) softened butter. Line the base and sides of the mould with baking parchment so it extends 12cm (5in) above the top.

7 Knead 100g (3½oz) softened butter, egg yolks, sugar, citrus peel, sultanas, nutmeg, lemon and orange zests, and vanilla extract into the dough until thoroughly combined, about 5 minutes (see page 99).

8 Shape the dough into a round loaf (see page 54). Place in the prepared mould. Use the tip of a sharp knife to cut an "X" across the top. Cover with a tea towel and prove until doubled in size, about 2 hours.

9 Brush the loaf with the egg glaze. Bake in the preheated oven for 45 minutes until a metal skewer inserted into the centre comes out clean. Remove from the mould and leave to cool in the lining paper on a wire rack. Dust with icing sugar.

To begin
Sponge method
Time: 20 minutes
(see page 44)

Rising
1 hour
(see pages 50–51)

Proving
2 hours
(see page 57)

Oven temperature
180°C/350°F/gas 4

Baking
45 minutes

Yield
1 loaf

Yeast alternative
20g (¾oz)
fresh yeast
(see page 41)

RECIPES USING BREAD

OWN THE AGES resourceful cooks have transformed breads into delicious sweet and savoury dishes and, although often born out of good housekeeping, many are now treasured as national favourites. These dishes usually evolved around the breads that were locally available: frugal Tuscan peasants stirred hearty country breads into soups and salads to make filling fare; thrifty British housewives incorporated tin loaves into sweet puddings; and great French chefs modelled light, white breads into golden, crispy garnishes for their haute cuisine creations.

BRUSCHETTA
GRILLED COUNTRY BREAD WITH GARLIC AND OLIVE OIL

Originally a Roman speciality, Bruschetta is now eaten throughout Italy. In Tuscany, during the olive harvest, thick slices of bread are grilled and then liberally anointed with the new season's olive oil.

INGREDIENTS

4 slices day-old country bread

1 garlic clove, peeled and cut in half

4 tbsp olive oil

coarse salt

1 Toast each of the bread slices on a preheated grill (either an outdoor barbecue or an oven grill).

2 While still hot, rub each slice of bread all over on one side with the cut side of the garlic clove.

3 Sprinkle olive oil and salt evenly over the bread slices. Serve hot. For a hearty alternative, top the grilled and seasoned slices of bread with crushed, ripe tomatoes and freshly torn basil leaves.

 Makes
4 servings

BREADS TO USE

Broa, page 78

Pane di Semola, page 87

Pane di Prato, page 88

Pane Casalingo, page 89

Ciabatta, page 90

PAPPA AL POMODORO CON PORRI
BREAD SOUP WITH TOMATOES AND LEEKS

A coarse country bread made with olive oil, such as Mantovana or Ciabatta, is best suited for this hearty Tuscan soup. Although fresh tomatoes are preferable, canned tomatoes make a suitable alternative. Serve this soup with a spoonful or two of freshly grated Parmesan cheese, a non-traditional but nonetheless delicious garnish to the recipe.

INGREDIENTS

2 tbsp olive oil

1 onion, peeled and finely chopped

4 slim or 2 fat leeks, finely chopped

1 garlic clove, peeled and crushed

½ tsp hot red pepper flakes

750g (1½lb) ripe tomatoes, chopped

1 litre (1¾ pints) hot chicken or vegetable stock

6 slices day-old country bread

6 basil leaves, torn

salt and freshly ground black pepper

4 tbsp extra virgin olive oil, to serve

1 Heat the oil in a large sauté pan. Add the onion and cook over a medium heat until golden and soft, about 5 minutes. Add the leeks, garlic, and red pepper flakes. Continue to cook until the leeks are soft and wilted, a further 5 minutes.

2 Stir in the tomatoes and cook until they begin to release their juices, about 5 minutes. Pour in the hot stock and bring to the boil. Season with salt and pepper and simmer gently for 30 minutes.

3 Cut the bread into 2.5cm (1in) cubes. Stir the bread into the hot soup and cook for a further 10 minutes until the bread is swollen and the soup has thickened.

4 Stir in the basil leaves. Check the seasoning, and add more salt and pepper if necessary. Serve in warmed bowls, with the extra virgin olive oil.

 Makes
4 servings

BREADS TO USE

Pain Ordinaire, page 72

Broa, page 78

Pain de Campagne, page 85

San Francisco Sourdough, page 86

Pane di Semola, page 87

Pane di Prato, page 88

Pane Casalingo, page 89

Ciabatta, page 90

Mantovana, page 114

PANZANELLA
TUSCAN BREAD AND TOMATO SALAD

In Tuscan farmhouse kitchens, Panzanella is made at the end of the summer to use up the seasonal glut of tomatoes, cucumbers, and basil. In Tuscany, the bread used is Pane di Prato, a coarse, saltless bread, but any open-textured country bread will do. Fresh, but very ripe, red tomatoes are essential. Leave tomatoes to ripen on a sunny windowsill.

INGREDIENTS

6 slices day-old country bread

1kg (2lb) fresh, ripe tomatoes, skinned and seeded

½ cucumber, peeled

125g (4oz) black olives, pitted and halved

1 red onion, peeled and finely chopped

2 tbsp capers, rinsed

6 basil leaves, torn

90ml (3fl oz) extra virgin olive oil

30ml (1fl oz) white wine vinegar

salt and freshly ground black pepper

1 Cut the bread into 1.5cm (½in) cubes and put them in a large bowl. Dice the tomatoes and cucumber and add to the bowl with the olives, onion, capers, and basil.

2 Add the olive oil and vinegar and season with salt and pepper. Stir well, then leave for 1 hour at room temperature to allow the flavours to blend well.

3 Toss everything together thoroughly. Check the seasoning, and add more salt and pepper, if necessary, before serving.

Makes
4 servings

BREADS TO USE

*Pain de Campagne,
page 85*

*San Francisco Sourdough,
page 86*

Pane di Prato, page 88

Pane Casalingo, page 89

Ciabatta, page 90

PAIN PERDU
FRENCH TOAST

Pain Perdu – *literally "lost bread" – is so called because the bread is so smothered in an egg-and-milk custard that it disappears altogether, and is thus lost. In France, this favourite family leftover dish is usually served with jam, but we also love it American-style, with crispy bacon and maple syrup.*

INGREDIENTS
2 eggs, beaten

300ml (½ pint) milk

75g (2½oz) caster sugar

8 slices day-old bread

125g (4oz) unsalted butter

1 Place the eggs, milk, and 1 tablespoon of the sugar in a large bowl. Beat them together with a fork until thoroughly mixed and foaming. Pass the mixture through a fine sieve to remove any strands of egg white.

2 Dip the bread slices in the egg mixture, submerging each slice to coat it well.

3 Melt half the butter in a large, non-stick frying pan over a medium heat. When the butter begins to foam, add the slices, a few at a time, and fry until golden on both sides. Drain on kitchen towels.

4 Add the remaining butter to the pan as it is needed. Sprinkle the fried bread with the remaining sugar immediately and serve warm.

Makes
4 servings

BREADS TO USE
Victorian Milk Bread, page 76

Ballymaloe Brown Bread, page 78

Baguette, page 79

Brioche, page 112

Challah, page 150

BROWN BREAD ICE CREAM

A *popular dessert during the Victorian era in England, this crunchy-textured, caramel ice cream has recently been rediscovered. Brown Bread Ice Cream is best eaten when freshly made, but if you do make it in advance, remove it from the freezer and allow to soften for an hour in the refrigerator before serving. Serve with raspberries and garnish with a sprig of mint.*

INGREDIENTS
125g (4oz) fresh wholemeal breadcrumbs

125g (4oz) granulated sugar

90ml (3fl oz) water

500ml (17fl oz) double or whipping cream

75g (2½oz) icing sugar, sifted

1 tsp vanilla extract

2 tbsp dark rum, brandy, or whisky

1 Spread the breadcrumbs in an even layer on a baking sheet. Toast in the preheated oven, stirring occasionally, until crisp and golden brown, about 15 minutes.

2 Heat the sugar and the water in a saucepan over a low heat and stir gently. When the sugar has dissolved completely to form a syrup, raise the heat and boil rapidly until it starts to brown around the edge of the pan. Swirl the pan occasionally so that the syrup colours evenly to a rich brown. Take the pan from the heat and stir in the toasted breadcrumbs.

3 Turn the caramel-coated crumbs out on to a baking sheet lined with baking parchment and leave to cool until the crumbs have hardened.

4 Wrap the baking parchment around the caramel-coated crumbs. Crush the crumbs into small pieces with your hands.

5 Use a hand-held mixer or balloon whisk to whip the cream until it is soft and light. Fold the icing sugar, vanilla extract, and rum into the cream. Fold in the caramel-coated crumbs.

6 Turn out the mixture into a 750ml (1¼ pint), airtight plastic container, seal, and freeze overnight. Do not use an ice-cream machine. The churning motion will curdle the cream. Soften in the refrigerator for 1 hour before serving.

Oven temperature
220°C/425°F/gas 7

Baking
15 minutes

Makes
4–6 servings

BREADS TO USE
Pain Ordinaire made with brown flour, page 72

Granary Tin Loaf, page 73

Ballymaloe Brown Bread, page 78

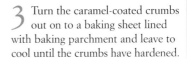

BREAD & BUTTER PUDDING

This old-fashioned favourite was originally made with leftover, plain white or brown bread, but *Victorian Milk Bread Brioche, Challah,* or *Panettone can be used for more indulgent versions. Try the chocolate variation for a wickedly delicious pudding. Make with any of the breads suggested or try it with Cinnamon Raisin Bread for a real treat. Soak the raisins in dark rum for a lusciously boozy twist – Chocolate, Rum, and Raisin Bread Pudding.*

INGREDIENTS

32 slices Baguette, or 8 slices tin loaf

30g (1oz) unsalted butter, softened

100g (3½oz) raisins

zest of 1 lemon, grated

¼ tsp ground nutmeg, plus extra to dust

3 eggs, beaten

3 tbsp caster sugar

500ml (17fl oz) milk

125ml (3½fl oz) double cream

1 tsp vanilla extract

icing sugar, to dust

1 Butter each slice of bread on one side. If using tin loaf slices, cut each one in half diagonally, then into quarters. Scatter 1 tablespoon of raisins over the bottom of a buttered, 1 litre (1¾ pint), oval baking dish.

2 Layer the buttered bread in the baking dish, sprinkling raisins, lemon zest, and nutmeg between each layer. Make sure that the top layer of bread is placed with the buttered side up.

3 Put the eggs and 2 tablespoons of the sugar in a large bowl. Heat the milk, cream, and vanilla extract in a saucepan over a medium heat, until just boiling. Whisk the hot milk and cream mixture into the eggs and sugar to make a custard; pour over the bread. Lightly press down the bread slices to completely submerge them in the custard.

4 Dust with nutmeg and 1 tablespoon of sugar. Cover the baking dish with a piece of greaseproof paper. Leave to soak for 20–30 minutes.

5 Bake in the preheated oven, covered, for 20 minutes. Remove the paper from the pudding and bake for a further 20–25 minutes until the custard has just set, the pudding has risen up slightly, and the bread slices have turned crispy around the edges. Dust with icing sugar and serve warm.

VARIATION
Chocolate Bread Pudding

• Make one quantity Bread & Butter Pudding up to step 2.

• Omit the lemon zest and replace the nutmeg with 1 teaspoon ground cinnamon. Arrange the bread in the dish as directed in step 2, sprinkling the raisins, cinnamon, and 100g (3½oz) plain chocolate, roughly chopped, between each layer.

• Put the eggs and sugar in a large bowl. Heat the milk, cream, and vanilla as directed in step 3; remove from the heat and add 100g (3½oz) chopped chocolate. Leave to stand for 5 minutes, then whisk until the chocolate has completely melted.

• Whisk the chocolate mixture into the eggs and sugar, then pour over the bread. Press the bread slices down into the mixture. Omitting the nutmeg, soak, bake, and serve, as directed in steps 4–5.

Oven temperature
220°C/425°F/gas 7

Baking
40–45 minutes

Makes
4–6 servings

BREADS TO USE

Pain Ordinaire, page 72

Victorian Milk Bread, page 76

Ballymaloe Brown Bread, page 78

Baguette, page 79

Brioche, page 112

Zopf, page 117

Pain Viennois, page 117

Challah, page 150

Pulla, page 150

Panettone, page 155

BREADCRUMBS & CROUTONS

BREADS TO USE FOR BREADCRUMBS

•

BREADS TO USE FOR CROUTES

•

BREADS TO USE FOR DICED CROUTONS

•

BREADS TO USE FOR MELBA TOAST

•

BREADS TO USE FOR SHAPED CROUTONS

SHAPED CROUTONS

LA CHAPELURE

DRIED BREADCRUMBS

The primary use of dried breadcrumbs is as a coating for ingredients to be deep-fried or roasted. Foods to be fried are usually dipped first in flour and then in beaten egg before being dipped in breadcrumbs. Ingredients such as fish fillets or rack of lamb are often spread with a little smooth mustard before the breadcrumbs are pressed on. Stored in an airtight container, dried breadcrumbs keep indefinitely.

Makes 125g (4oz) dried breadcrumbs

125g (4oz) slices day-old bread, crusts cut off

Put the bread slices on a baking sheet. Leave in a 150°C/ 300°F/gas 2 oven until dry and crisp, about 10 minutes. Let cool.
To grind by hand Wrap the bread in a plastic bag. Press a rolling pin all over the bag, crushing the bread until ground to the desired consistency. Press through a sieve for a finer texture.
To grind in a food processor or blender Put the dried bread in the work bowl of a food processor, or in a blender. Pulse to grind to the desired consistency.

VARIATION
Chapelure à la Provençale
• Make one quantity dried breadcrumbs.
• In a small bowl combine the dried breadcrumbs with 2 finely chopped garlic cloves, 3 tablespoons olive oil, 1 tablespoon fresh thyme leaves, a pinch each salt and pepper, and 4 tablespoons chopped parsley.
• Use to coat meat or fish before sprinkling with olive oil and roasting or grilling at a high temperature.

LA PANURE

FRESH BREADCRUMBS

Fresh breadcrumbs have two main roles. In stuffings, forcemeats, dumplings, and steamed puddings, breadcrumbs bind the ingredients together. When sprinkled as a topping over gratins and other baked dishes, breadcrumbs provide both colour and crunch and serve to protect creamy sauces from the high heat of the oven or grill. Fresh breadcrumbs can be stored in an air-tight container and frozen for up to six months.

Makes 150g (5oz) fresh breadcrumbs

150g (5oz) slices fresh bread, crusts cut off

To chop by hand Use a chef's knife to cut the bread into cubes on a large chopping board. Chop the bread cubes coarsely or finely as stipulated in the recipe.
To grind in a food processor or blender Cut the bread into rough chunks; put in the work bowl of a food processor, or a blender. Pulse the machine to grind the bread to the desired consistency.

VARIATIONS
Panure à la Milanaise
• Make one quantity fresh breadcrumbs.
• Mix with 60g (2oz) grated Parmesan.
• Use to top gratin dishes before baking or grilling at a high temperature.

Buttered Crumbs
• Make one quantity fresh breadcrumbs.
• Melt 60g (2oz) butter in a pan over a medium heat. When the butter is hot, add the breadcrumbs and stir well to coat evenly. Sauté until golden, about 1 minute.
• Use to top steamed vegetables.

CROUTES

Croûtes *make ideal canapé bases for savoury toppings like fresh goat's cheese. They are also an essential component of the classic, Parisian, bistro-style recipe* Soupe à L'Ognion Gratinée. Crostini *are simply the Italian (originally Tuscan) equivalent of the French* Croûtes.

Makes about 32 croûtes

1 day-old Baguette

Preheat the oven to 180°C/ 350°F/gas 4. Cut the Baguette into 1cm (½in) slices. Place slices in a single layer on a baking sheet. Bake until crisp, about 15 minutes. Use for canapé bases or with antipasti.

VARIATIONS
Cheese Croûtes
• Make one quantity Croûtes as directed.
• Melt 30g (1oz) butter. Grate 30g (1oz) Parmesan. Brush one side of each croûte with the butter or alternatively with oil.
• Sprinkle the grated cheese and a pinch of cayenne pepper evenly over the buttered side of each croûte. Place in a single layer on a baking sheet and bake for 5 minutes more, until golden.
• Use as a garnish for soups or salads.

Garlic Croûtes
• Make one quantity Croûtes as directed.
• Peel 1 garlic clove and cut it in half.
• Rub one side of each croûte with the cut side of the garlic. Sprinkle this side of each of the croûtes with olive oil.
• Use as a garnish for soups or salads.

DICED CROUTONS

Diced Croûtons *add a delicious crunch to soups, salads, and omelettes. They are best when made just before serving, but may be prepared several hours ahead and kept at room temperature. To reheat, place in an oven, 160°C/325°F/gas 3, for 5 minutes.*

Makes about 40 croûtons

4 slices day-old bread, crusts cut off

30g unsalted butter and 2 tbsp sunflower oil

To fry Cut the bread into 1cm (½in) cubes. Heat the butter and oil in a frying pan over a low heat. Test that it is hot enough by adding one cube to the pan; the bread should sizzle when it goes in. Place the cubes in the pan in a single layer. Sauté, stirring constantly, for about 10 minutes until crisp. Drain on kitchen towels before serving. Leave to cool.

Makes about 40 croûtons

4 slices day-old bread, crusts cut off

30g unsalted butter, melted

To bake Preheat the oven to 200°C/400°F/gas 6. Cut the bread into 1cm (½in) cubes; place in a roasting dish. Pour the melted butter over the cubes and toss them to coat evenly. Bake until crisp and golden, about 10 minutes.

VARIATION
Garlic Croûtons
• Make one quantity Diced Croûtons by either method as directed; remove from the frying pan or oven just before they are done.
• Toss with 1 finely chopped garlic clove while still hot and before draining.
• Return to a hot frying pan or oven for a couple of minutes to finish crispening.

MELBA TOAST

These wafer-thin slices of toast make a perfect accompaniment to pâtés, potted meats, creamy dips and, best of all, caviar. They can be stored in an airtight container for several days; reheat before serving.

Makes about 32 toasts

4 slices bread, each about 1cm (½in) thick

Preheat the oven to 180°C/ 350°F/gas 4. Toast the bread slices. Cut off the crusts and slice each piece of toast in half horizontally to make two slices from one. Cut each slice in half diagonally and in half again to make small triangle shapes. Place on a baking sheet and bake for 10 minutes until golden, crisp, and curled.

SHAPED CROUTONS

These elegant, parsley-tipped shapes are used in French haute cuisine *as a classic garnish.*

Makes about 12 heart-shaped croûtons

4 slices bread, each about ½cm (¼in) thick

30g (1oz) unsalted butter

2 tbsp sunflower oil

1 tbsp finely chopped parsley, optional

Cut the bread into heart-shaped pieces. Heat the butter and oil in a frying pan over a low heat. Add the bread shapes to the pan in a single layer. Sauté for about 5 minutes on each side until golden. If desired, dip the pointed ends of the croutons in the finely chopped parsley.

PROBLEM SOLVING

A LESS THAN PERFECT LOAF of bread generally begins with a less than perfect dough. In fact, the most common mistake in breadmaking is producing a dough that is too dry. A dry dough is stiff and hard and will remain a solid, heavy lump that will resist proper kneading, rising, proving, and shaping. It is impossible to specify an exact quantity of liquid, or indeed precise rising times, for each recipe when flour, temperature, and humidity vary so greatly from kitchen to kitchen, and region to region. Carefully follow the recipe instructions for dough consistency, as well as the kneading, rising, and proving times. However, remember that bread dough is influenced by its environment. Therefore, it is important to take this factor into account and adjust the instructions as necessary. Use these guidelines to help make a perfect dough.

ACHIEVING THE RIGHT CONSISTENCY

THE IDEAL CONSISTENCY for most doughs is firm but moist. A dough should feel soft and slightly sticky after mixing, but should become smooth and elastic as it is kneaded. Resist adding extra flour until you are certain that the dough is unmanageable. Adjustments are best made at the mixing stage, but additional water or flour can be added to the dough at the kneading stage as well.

DRY DOUGH AT THE MIXING STAGE

1 The bulk of the flour and the water gathers together into a ball but also leaves a crumbly mass at the bottom of the mixing bowl. Add water, 1 teaspoon at a time, to the dry crumbs.

2 Use a wooden spoon to mix the dry crumbs with the water until a smooth paste is formed. Combine this mixture with the main bulk of the dough by kneading the two together with your hands.

DRY DOUGH AT THE KNEADING STAGE

THE DOUGH HAS BEEN gathered to form a ball but is still too stiff and hard to knead. Add water gradually to allow the dough to absorb the liquid without becoming a slippery, sticky mess. A water sprayer with a fine mist is best for this purpose. Spray the dough and continue kneading; repeat until you achieve the required consistency. If you do not have a water sprayer, moisten your hands lightly with water and knead. Repeat, if necessary.

WET DOUGH AT THE KNEADING STAGE

THE DOUGH IS REQUIRED to be firm enough to hold its shape after kneading. In most recipes it should become more pliable as it is kneaded: your fingers should come away as you knead and it should feel smooth and light. However, if the dough is still too wet to work with, extra flour can be added at the kneading stage. Dust the dough lightly with flour and continue kneading; dust again with more flour, only if necessary.

COMMON PROBLEMS IN BAKED BREADS

PROBLEM	POSSIBLE CAUSES	REMEDIES
CLOSE-TEXTURED, DENSE CRUMB	• The dough was too dry. It should feel soft and sticky after mixing. If dry, it will not develop.	• *Follow the instructions to achieve the required dough consistency given in the recipe. See instructions on the opposite page for adding additional liquid at either the mixing or the kneading stage.*
	• The dough was not sufficiently kneaded. It should feel smooth and elastic after kneading.	• *To test the dough for sufficient kneading, press it with a fingertip. The indent made with your finger should spring back immediately. If it does not, continue to knead until it is ready.*
	• The dough had not risen sufficiently. It should rise until it is doubled in size, puffy, and aerated.	• *Check the dough after rising to be sure that it has risen properly. Use the test illustrated below to determine if more time is necessary.* • *To ensure that rising is complete, test the dough by gently pressing it with a fingertip (see right). If the dough has risen properly it will not spring back completely. The dough will spring back at once if the rising is not complete.*
A FLAT AND SPREAD-OUT LOAF	• The dough was over-proved, causing the loaf to collapse from the initial exposure to the heat of the oven during baking. When dough is very puffed up and more than doubled in size (unless specified in the recipe) it is over-proved.	• *Knock the shaped dough back, reshape it, and leave to prove again. If the recipe requires the dough to be so soft that it does not hold its shape, use a basket to support the loaf while proving.* • *To test for over-proving press the dough with a fingertip. If the dough has been over-proved it will deflate and release a strong smell of fermenting yeast.*
CRACKS ON SIDES OF LOAF	• The dough was under-proved, causing the loaf to expand too much in the oven. The loaf burst open during baking after the outer crust had already formed.	• *Leave the shaped dough to prove until it has doubled in volume and is light, puffy, and aerated. Test the dough for sufficient proving by gently pressing it with a fingertip – if the dough does not form an indentation or springs back quickly it requires more proving time. If an indentation is made and then springs back gradually but completely, the dough is ready to be placed in the oven.*
	• The dough was improperly shaped or the seam was not sealed well at the end of shaping.	• *Review basic shaping (see pages 52–57). Be sure to always apply pressure evenly at the various steps of shaping a loaf and to allow the dough to rest in between steps should it begin to resist or tighten.*
DRY PATCHES OF UNCOOKED DOUGH	• The dough was left either uncovered or in a draughty place during the rising or the proving steps of the recipe.	• *Cover the dough securely with a tea towel (see right) and avoid draughty places while rising and proving. Discard any dry, crusty pieces that have formed on top of the dough before shaping.*

GLOSSARY

Anise seeds green-brown, oval seeds with an aromatic liquorice flavour. Native to the Middle East, anise seeds are widely available in most supermarkets.

Batter a mixture of flour, liquid, and sometimes leaven that can be thick or thin, but is of spooning or pouring consistency.

Biga Italian for a starter. Traditionally fermented for a minimum of 12 hours, it produces a bread with a lightly fermented taste, and an open, porous texture.

Boule French for ball, referring to a round loaf of white bread also called *miche*.

Bread dough a mixture of flour, liquid, and often leaven, used to make bread. The required consistency of bread dough varies according to the recipe instructions and the desired texture and appearance of the loaf, but it should generally be stiff enough to work easily with the hands.

Brioche traditional French bread dough enriched with butter and eggs. The classic shape, called *Brioche à Tête*, is round and has a fluted base and a top knot.

Brot the German word for bread.

Buttermilk an ingredient made by adding special bacteria to skimmed or semi-skimmed milk, giving it a slightly thickened texture and tangy flavour. If unavailable, it can be substituted with the following mixture: 1 tablespoon lemon juice or cider vinegar, plus enough semi-skimmed milk to make up 250ml (8oz). Stir, then let stand for 5 minutes. This will yield 250ml (8fl oz).

Chafe to shape a risen dough into a round by using your hands to apply a downwards pressure to the sides of the dough while at the same time rotating it at the base.

Crust the hardened outer layer of, most commonly, a cooked food such as bread.

Dough a stiff but pliable mixture of flour, liquid, and other ingredients. This mixture remains a dough until it has been baked.

Fermentation a process during which carbohydrates go through a chemical change caused by enzymes produced from bacteria, micro-organisms, or yeast.

Ghee a term for concentrated, clarified butter with a strong, sweet flavour, used as a cooking fat in India and many Arab countries.

Gluten the stretchy elastic strands of protein that form when wheat flour is mixed with water and kneaded. It causes a bread dough to rise by trapping the carbon dioxide given off by the yeast and creates a network of bubbles in the crumb of the baked loaf.

Grease to prepare a bread tin or mould by brushing the inside with oil or butter before adding a dough or batter. This prevents the bread from sticking during baking.

Herbes de Provence an aromatic blend of dried herbs that grow in the Provence region of France; these usually include thyme, rosemary, bay, basil, savory, marjoram, lavender, and fennel seeds. It is available in speciality stores and some supermarkets.

Jalapeño a dark green variety of chilli that may vary from medium hot to very hot in flavour. Measures about 5cm (2in) long and 2cm (1in) wide, and has a rounded tip.

Key a term used to describe the final seam produced in a piece of dough once it has been folded and shaped into a loaf.

Kirsch a clear fruit brandy distilled from whole cherries. Used both as a digestive liqueur and as a flavouring in baking.

Knead to work a dough by rhythmically pushing, stretching, and folding it in order to develop the gluten in the flour.

Knock back to deflate a fully risen dough by pressing down on it and literally forcing the air out before the dough is shaped.

Leaven an agent such as yeast or baking powder that is added to baked goods to lighten the texture and increase the volume.

Leavened a word describing baked goods that contain a rising agent.

Linseeds also known as flax seeds, these tiny, oval, shiny brown seeds are rich in nutrients and are available from health-food stores.

Nigella seeds available in Middle Eastern, Indian, and other speciality stores, these tiny black seeds with a nutty flavour are sometimes called black onion seeds.

Orange-flower water distilled from fresh orange blossoms, this perfumed flavouring is available in Middle Eastern, Indian, and other speciality stores.

Pain the French word for bread.

Pane the Italian word for bread.

Paste a mixture of flour, liquid, and sometimes a leaven, which is too stiff to pour but too moist to work with the hands.

Poolish French for a starter. Traditionally fermented for a minimum of 2 hours, it produces a bread with a light, springy texture and a nutty aroma.

Prosciutto also sold under the name Parma Ham, this unsmoked, Italian ham has been pressed, salt-cured, and air-dried.

Proving also referred to as the final rise, this is the process during which a shaped dough is left to rise just before baking.

Rising the process during which a dough is aerated by carbon dioxide gas produced by a leavening agent before and during baking, causing it to grow in volume.

Sift to pass dry ingredients through a fine sieve in order to incorporate air and to make them lighter and more even in texture.

Slash to make incisions in the surface of a risen dough before baking to allow the loaf to rise and expand as it bakes without tearing or cracking the outer crust.

Sourdough, Sourdough bread a bread with a slightly sour, tangy flavour created by using a sourdough starter as the leaven.

Sourdough starter (see Starter) a starter that has been left to ferment for at least 48 hours. It produces a bread with a unique, slightly sour, tangy flavour.

Sponging the process by which a period of fermentation is added during the mixing stage, to produce a bread with a light crumb and a faintly yeasty aroma.

Star Anise available in Asian and speciality stores, this star-shaped spice has a strong, sweet aniseed flavour. It is a key ingredient in Chinese five-spice powder.

Starter a mixture of flour, yeast, and water, left to ferment for 2 hours to 5 days, and up to 2 weeks. It is used as an alternative rising agent to yeast, on its own, to leaven a bread dough. It is added to the flour at the mixing step when making a bread dough and affects both the taste and texture of bread.

Unleavened a word describing baked foods that contain no rising agent.

INDEX

USEFUL ADDRESSES

Speciality Flour Suppliers
Marriage's Flour,
Chelmsford Chelmer Mills
and Brick Barns Farm Ltd.,
Chelmsford,
Essex CM1 1PN
Tel: 01245 354455
www.marriagefeeds.co.uk
Mail order service.

Shipton Mill,
Long Newnton,
Tetbury,
Gloucester GL8 8RP
Tel: 01666 505050
www.shipton-mill.com
Mail order service.

Dove's Farm,
Salisbury Road,
Hungerford,
Berkshire RG17 0RF
Tel: 01488 684880
www.dovesfarm.co.uk
Mail order service.

Little Salkeld Watermill,
Penrith,
Cumbria CA10 1NN
Tel: 01768 881523
www.organicmill.co.uk
Mail order service.

**Information on Flour and
Breadmaking**
Flour Advisory Bureau Ltd.,
21 Arlington Street,
London SW1A 1RN
Tel: 020 7493 2521
www.fabflour.co.uk

**Speciality Breadmaking
Equipment**
Divertimenti,
33–34 Marylebone High St.,
London W1U 4PT
Tel: 020 7935 0689
and 227–229 Brompton Rd,
London SW3 2EP
Tel: 020 7581 8065
www.divertimenti.co.uk
Mail order service.

Alan Silverwood Ltd.,
Ledsam Street,
Ledsam House,
Birmingham B16 8DN
Tel: 0121 454 3571
silverbake@aol.com

French Baguette Trays
David Mellor,
4 Sloane Square,
London SW1 8EE
Tel: 020 7730 4259
Tel: 01433 650 220 (HQ)
www.davidmellordesign.com
davidmellor@ukonline.co.uk
Mail order service.

**Spices and Speciality
Ingredients**
The Spice Shop,
1 Blenheim Crescent,
London W11 2EE
Tel: 020 7221 4448
www.thespiceshop.co.uk
info@thespiceshop.co.uk
Mail order service.

**Breadmaking Classes for
Adults and Children**
Books For Cooks,
4 Blenheim Crescent,
London W11 1NN
Tel: 020 7221 1992
www.booksforcooks.com
info@booksforcooks.com

ACKNOWLEDGMENTS

AUTHORS' ACKNOWLEDGMENTS
It may only take a little time to make an honest loaf, but this book would not have been possible without the help, patience, understanding, passion, and support of a number of people.

Eric Treuille would like to thank Julia Pemberton Hellums for keeping everything together and for invaluable information about American breads and flours, Julia Brock for helping with German breads, and Didier Lascaze, my wonderful traditional baker and friend in Cahors, for helping me immeasurably to understand real breadmaking. Heidi Lascelles who is always there for us with support, love, and enthusiasm for all enterprises at Books For Cooks, whether it be late-night recipe testing and tasting, baking workshops, or teaching nursery school children the basics of breadmaking. Peter and Juliet Kindersley for the use of their kitchen, weekend after weekend, for bringing us back breads from their travels all over the world, and for allowing the collaboration of the "ladies" in the arduous task of quality control. The DK and studio teams for their creativity, energy, and good will in this especially challenging project. Ursula for never letting us down with her enthusiasm

and driving passion for this book and everything to do with breadmaking. Finally, special thanks to my wife Rose, because she made this book not just possible, but the ultimate of its kind.

Ursula Ferrigno would like to thank Julia Pemberton Hellums for her outstanding editing and dedication to our book. I am thrilled for her total involvement every step of the way, and for her encouragement and persistence for a great result. Rosie Kindersley, not only for her excellent eye but also for her determination for this book to be better than any other; her researching and energy are boundless. Ian O'Leary: it has been so delightful working with him in his fabulous studio and with Emma, his assistant – his photographs are amazing. Hilary Krag and Gurinder Purewall, for their great design work. My family, as always, for their power of listening and advice and help with research. My man in Rome for just being him, and his help with my dreadful spelling. Kate O'Donnel for recipe testing so diligently in the heat of the summer. Books For Cooks for allowing me to be there for all the fun and support, particularly Heidi Lascelles the owner. My co-author for his determination and amazing food-styling eye.

PUBLISHER'S ACKNOWLEDGMENTS
Dorling Kindersley would like to thank Neff U.K. Ltd. for the use of one of their ovens, Kitchen Aid for the donation of their appliances, Shipton Mills for their generous donations of flour and plant specimens, The Flour Advisory Board for help with flour research, Nicola Nieburg for editorial assistance, Susan Bosanko for the index, Christine Rista for picture research, and make-up artist Sue Sian.

Picture Credits
Key to pictures: t = top, c = centre, b = bottom, l = left, r = right.

The publisher would like to thank the following for their kind permission to reproduce the following photographs: Musée de la Ville de Paris, Musée Carnavalet, Paris 12tl;
Mary Evans Picture Library 16tl;
AKG London 18tl;
Dover Publications 22tl;
Ann Ronan Picture Library 24tl.

Photography by Ian O'Leary, except: David Murray and Jules Selmes 27c;
Martin Cameron 34tr;
Clive Streeter 99cl, 101r;
Steve Gorton 99cl;
Dave King 115cr;
Philip Dowell 144br.